Praise for *Preachers at Prayer*

"*Preachers at Prayer* is a book that helps the reader understand more deeply what is stated so powerfully in John 1:18: *Only the one who comes from the breast of the Father can make him known.* This book is a must-read for all the members of the Dominican family and for all those who desire to share the warmth of God's love that they know and feel in their hearts."

—**Gerard Timoner, OP**, Master of the Order of Preachers, from the foreword

"*Preachers at Prayer* is a moving invitation to every preacher. Fr. Murray shows that it is in quiet prayer that preachers find—or rather, are given—these essential elements that light fire both in their hearts and in the hearts of hearers: spiritual depth, from preachers who have surrendered themselves to the Gospel of Christ; delight in God and in God's beloved; wisdom and integrity, fruits of the cross of Christ in which preachers lovingly share; compassion for God's people, which shines not only in words spoken but first and foremost in lived, visible witness; and hope—the piercing conviction that God is ever-faithful, and that his Word, Jesus, is himself the fullness of truth. Fr. Murray offers every preacher profound insight from the great teachers of the Dominican spiritual tradition and thus invites us to lean deeply, in love and surrender, into the side of Christ and into the heart of the Church. A striking quotation from Bl. Humbert of Romans will stay with me as a permanent, stirring challenge: 'If preaching fails, there is spiritual famine.'"

—**Archbishop J. Peter Sartain**, Archbishop Emeritus of Seattle

"This much-needed book by revered spiritual master Paul Murray, OP, responds to a concern of Pope Francis that people 'suffer because of homilies.' With erudition and eloquence, Fr. Murray encourages preachers to harness the 'intelligence of the faith' so that, in preaching, they can devote closer attention to the 'void or gap in our lives,' 'that ache for God familiar to us all, our heart's wound of longing.' Preaching is to be focused 'on the drama of divine mercy'; it must pass on 'a personal and living experience of the mystery' (Pope St. John Paul II) and 'awaken new desire for God and new hope.' For 'if preaching fails, there is spiritual famine' (Bl. Humbert of Romans). This book provides nourishment that leads to a feast."

—**Peter John Cameron, OP**, Carl J. Peter Chair of Homiletics, Pontifical North American College, Rome

"*Preachers at Prayer* is a rare gift. Although it is a collection of Paul Murray's addresses to Dominicans, it allows the rest of us who must also proclaim the Gospel to eavesdrop and so learn vital lessons about prayer, about study, and about that darkness that is caused not by obscurity but by the radiance of God's presence. Learning these lessons will change us. This rare gift is for everyone."

—**Msgr. Roderick Strange**, Professor of Theology at St. Mary's University, Twickenham (England), author of *Journey into Light*

PREACHERS *at* PRAYER

PREACHERS *at* PRAYER

Soundings in the Dominican Spiritual Tradition

PAUL MURRAY, OP

FOREWORD BY GERARD TIMONER, OP

Published by Word on Fire, Elk Grove Village, IL 60007
© 2024 by Paul Murray
Printed in the United States of America
All rights reserved

Cover design, typesetting, and interior art direction by Cassie Bielak

Cover image: *The Nine Ways of Prayer of Saint Dominic*,
Biblioteca Apostolica Vaticana, Ross. 3 (f. 9r)

Scripture excerpts are from the New Revised Standard Version Bible:
Catholic Edition (copyright © 1989, 1993), used by permission of the
National Council of the Churches of Christ in the United States of America.
All rights reserved worldwide.

Chapter 1, "Prayer into Preaching: Recovering the Contemplative Dimension,"
given originally as a talk to the General Chapter of the Dominican Order
(Providence, RI, July 2001). This talk was published as a small book by
Dominican Publications, Dublin, in 2003 (https://dominicanpublications.
com/). Chapter 2, "What Makes for Good Preaching?" given originally as a talk
to the International Colloquium on *Dei Verbum* (Angelicum, Rome, February
27, 2016). This talk, with its original title, "Preaching Today," was published in
Angelicum 93, no. 3 (2016): 585–598. Chapter 3, "Dominican Wisdom and the
Dark Night," given originally as an Aquinas Lecture, Dominican University
(River Forest, IL, February 28, 2008). Chapter 4, "Dominicans and the Key of
Knowledge," given originally as a talk for Dominican friars studying in Rome
on a day of retreat held at the Angelicum (February 19, 2023).

First printing, May 2024

ISBN: 978-1-68578-095-1

Library of Congress Control Number: 2023951023

Dedicated
to Philip McShane, OP

Contents

Foreword

Gerard Timoner, OP
Master of the Order of Preachers

Preachers at Prayer is a book addressed to "attentive seekers of truth, men and women of prayer, readers interested in learning more about the Dominican spiritual tradition." Brother Paul Murray, esteemed and beloved professor at the Angelicum and former spiritual director of the Convitto Internazionale San Tommaso, shares with a wider audience the gathered fruits of his contemplation—a collection of talks he gave over several years right up to the present, all of them delivered in *loving obedience* to his confreres and students who requested him to speak on the different themes that make up the chapters of the present work. Echoing the prophet Ezekiel, Paul wisely calls our attention to the "gaps" and fissures of our times, most notably the gap between praying and preaching. Drawing from the rich tradition of men and women who followed Christ the Preacher, the author invites the reader to see the golden link between contemplation and action, prayer and preaching, speaking *with* God and speaking *about* God.

St. Catherine of Siena's vision of St. Dominic emerging from the Father's breast is one of the striking images in the book. Dominic, as preacher and contemplative, is viewed by Catherine as someone who goes toward the world loved by God, instead of turning away from it. Like John the beloved disciple at the Last Supper, Dominic at prayer is someone who leans close to the chest of Jesus, *listening to the Lord's heartbeat* (John 13:23). And it is that *listening*, more than anything else, that inevitably quickens the passion to preach. Dominic, moved by the intimate knowledge gained of divine truth and divine love, feels at once compelled to share that knowledge with the world.

Preachers at Prayer is a book that helps the reader understand more deeply what is stated so powerfully in John 1:18: *Only the one who comes from the breast of the Father can make him known.* This book is a must-read for all the members of the Dominican family and for all those who desire to share the warmth of God's love that they know and feel in their hearts.

Introduction

The painter Vincent van Gogh, writing to his brother Theo in the summer of 1880, remarked: "There may be a great fire in our soul, but no one ever seems to come to warm himself at it, and the passers-by see only a little bit of smoke coming through the chimney and pass on their way."[1] These lines were penned by Van Gogh at the time when his work was being either quietly ignored by his contemporaries or else dismissed out of hand. The great artist was, of course, referring to his own work as a painter and not, therefore, to a conviction regarding the Christian Gospel. Nevertheless, for those who believe they have been called to preach the Word of God, these lines have an immediate resonance.

If the statement is applied to the work of preachers and evangelists today, the fire in the soul can be said to represent nothing less than the Gospel itself. Between this "fire" and contemporary culture, however, a fissure has opened, a rupture, which is impossible to ignore. What, then, needs to be done? Van Gogh, in his letter, offers the following calm, courageous advice. He writes, "[One must] tend that inward fire, have salt in oneself, and wait patiently yet with how much impatience for the hour when somebody will come and

---

1. Vincent van Gogh, *The Letters of Vincent van Gogh*, ed. Mark Roskill (London: Macmillan, 1963), 122.

sit down near it, to stay there maybe. Let him who believes in God wait for the hour that will come sooner or later."[2]

A powerful statement by any standard. But if its message is taken to heart by contemporary Christians, active preachers among them, it will obviously not be enough for them—for us—to sit down at the fire of our own convictions and wait for the world to come around to our point of view. We have not been given the fire of heaven for our own tribal comfort and consolation. We are not to behave as if the Good News were only good news for the righteous few and could never travel beyond the borders of an exclusive tribe or sect. No, as committed believers, we are called "to go up into the gaps" and to cast our fire into the midst.

That phrase, "go up into the gaps," will no doubt sound familiar to you. It comes from Ezekiel 13 and is one of the most challenging passages in the entire prophetic tradition. Speaking through his prophet, the Lord says of the preachers of that time, "You have not gone up into the gaps to build a wall for the house of Israel to stand in battle on the day of the LORD" (Ezek. 13:5 NKJV). If we take the implied imperative of Ezekiel—"go up into the gaps"—and apply it to our own age and situation, what is the most urgent, most critical message now being announced? Are there "gaps" that today are being ignored? Is there a front line, as it were, that we have not had the courage to face, a challenge that for years perhaps we have been avoiding?

Pope St. Paul VI, having in mind the gap that has opened, and opened wide, between the secular ideologies of our time and the Christian faith tradition, referred to it once, in a brief, vivid phrase,

2. Van Gogh, 122–123.

as "the drama of our time."[3] It is a gap that impacts every man and woman attempting, in a secular age, to follow the path of Christ. Its impact will be felt most especially by those who have been called to preach the Christian Gospel and who, as a result, find themselves standing at the front line as it were between, on the one hand, certain radical expressions of the Gospel tradition and, on the other hand, the forms and fashions of contemporary society.

At Vatican II, it was acknowledged that "the human race is passing through a new stage of its history." We were alerted to the fact that "profound and rapid changes" were spreading by degrees around the whole world.[4] So, faced with the gap, the fissure, between faith tradition and the secular world, one of the tasks set for us by the council was to seek continually for new and more effective ways of communicating the Gospel to the men and women of our time, an undertaking that would call for dynamic new initiatives. Needless to say, this task of "making it new," of going up into the gaps, remains still the great challenge facing us today. But, while seeking in every way possible to allow the Word of God to be heard by our contemporaries, we should, with no less determination, be devoting ever closer attention to that other void or gap in our lives, that inner space that may be no less challenging to confront, that ache for God familiar to us all, our heart's wound of longing.

When we attempt to go down to the root of our desire and wait on God, we may perhaps experience at first no awareness of the divine, but rather a great sense of emptiness. As a result, it is not always easy to remain there. But to remain there is precisely

3. Paul VI, *Evangelii Nuntiandi* 20, apostolic exhortation, December 8, 1975, vatican.va.
4. Second Vatican Council, preface to *Gaudium et Spes* 4, in *The Word on Fire Vatican II Collection*, ed. Matthew Levering (Park Ridge, IL: Word on Fire Institute, 2021), 217.

what the great tradition so often and so insistently recommends. "Stand still," Meister Eckhart is fond of repeating, "and do not waver from your emptiness."[5] Eckhart is well aware, of course, that many believers—many of us—are still somewhat frightened of that void within and are not always able to believe that God in fact supports us in our emptiness. We panic, and we find, perhaps unconsciously, a wonderful alibi by becoming absorbed in all kinds of projects and plans—*holy* projects, of course, and *holy* plans—anything so long as it will distract us from the void within. But our good works, our great plans for the future, and even our most imaginative projects are all so much "whitewash" (Ezekiel's phrase) if, at the core, they represent simply an escape from that inner void. *Stand still, and do not waver from your emptiness.*

Van Gogh's image of staying close to the fire that burns within is, I would suggest, a powerful, salutary image for ourselves today. Whatever new initiatives we undertake, whatever radical changes we make to serve those most in need of help, we are called to stay close to the fire of the Gospel, to the Word heard from the beginning, and to "tend that inward fire" and keep "salt" within ourselves. It goes without saying that the most obvious, most helpful way to keep that salt fresh and tend that inward fire is humble, consistent dedication to the practice of prayer.

That is, of course, what we witness in the lives of the Dominican preachers most celebrated in the tradition. They are men and women who have come to know by experience the true nature of God, and their hearts are on fire as a result. They cannot wait to share their discovery. They have dared to go down to the root of their desire,

5. Meister Eckhart, "Sermon 4," in *The Complete Mystical Works of Meister Eckhart*, ed. and trans. Maurice O'C. Walshe (New York: Crossroad, 1992), 59.

and—in the innermost gap of their own spirit—they have found courage to stand still and wait for the warmth, for the fire of the Spirit of God, to come upon them and to capture their hearts once and for all. Fire—the searching, consoling, energizing fire of God's infinite love.

The Dominican spiritual tradition, I'm happy to say, leaves us in no doubt that even the weakest disciple among us can, here and now, in faith if not in feeling, begin to experience something of this wonderful blessing. That is the good news that, in the chapters which follow, I now intend to explore.

* * *

All four chapters are based on talks that, over several years, I have been asked to give on the subjects of prayer, study, and preaching. But now, as I am about to publish these talks in book form, I am made piercingly aware of my presumption as an author. For, far from being a master of prayer, I am, if the truth be known, even at this late stage in life, no more than a novice. However, remembering with heartfelt gratitude the generous response of those who, over the years, attended these four talks, and the great joy I experienced in giving them, I am encouraged to think that maybe, in this newly published format, the talks might be of some use to others, preachers among them, attentive seekers of truth, men and women of prayer, readers interested in learning more about the Dominican spiritual tradition.

Prayer into Preaching[1]

Recovering the Contemplative Dimension

Although fidelity to the life of prayer and contemplation has been a distinguishing mark of the most celebrated Dominican preachers and saints, the Order itself has been noted, over the centuries, more for its intellectual prowess than for its contemplative zeal. Today, however, all that is beginning to change. There are now widely available, for example, many translations of the writings of people like Johannes Tauler, Catherine of Siena, Henry Suso, and Meister Eckhart. And St. Thomas Aquinas, who was always revered as a dogmatic theologian within the Church, is now being regarded also, by many people, as a spiritual master.

So, it would seem that, all of a sudden, there is an opportunity to enable the contemplative dimension of the Dominican tradition to speak with a new and telling authority to a new generation. Not all forms of contemplation, it has to be said, were affirmed by the early Friars Preachers. In fact, in the *Vitae Fratrum*, there has survived a vivid account of one unfortunate friar who very nearly lost his

---

1. A talk given originally to the General Chapter of the Dominican Order (Providence, RI, July 2001).

faith from too much "contemplation"![2] In similar vein, Humbert of Romans, in his long treatise on preaching, openly complains about those people whose "sole passion is for contemplation." These men seek out, he says, a "hidden life of quiet" or "a retired place for contemplation," and then "refuse to respond to the summons to be useful to others by preaching."[3] Now, obviously, Humbert of Romans is not intending somehow to set up as contraries to one another the life of prayer and the life of preaching. "Since human effort can achieve nothing without the help of God," he writes, "the most important thing of all for a preacher is that he should have recourse to prayer."[4] But the life of prayer and contemplation, which Humbert of Romans and the early Dominicans would recommend, is one that would compel us, in Humbert's phrase, to "come out into the open"[5]—compel us, that is, to set about the task of preaching.

To begin our reflections, I suggest we look first not to one of the most famous texts from the Dominican tradition but to a text by an anonymous French Dominican of the thirteenth century. The passage in question I found hidden away in a large biblical commentary on the book of Revelation that for centuries had been attributed to Aquinas. The work is now judged, however, to have been composed by a Dominican équipe working at Saint-Jacques in Paris under the general supervision of the Dominican Hugh of

---

2. Gerald de Frachet, *Vitae Fratrum* 3.15, in *Monumenta Ordinis Fratrum Praedicatorum Historica* [hereafter, MOFPH] 1, ed. B.M. Reichert (Louvain: Charpentier & Schoonjans, 1896), 112.

3. Humbert of Romans, "Treatise on the Formation of Preachers" 4.17.193. (Humbert is quoting from St. Gregory the Great's *Pastoral Rule*.) See *Early Dominicans: Selected Writings*, ed. Simon Tugwell (New York: Paulist, 1982), 242. I am happy here to express my gratitude to Simon for his work as editor and translator of many of the most important early Dominican texts.

4. "Treatise on the Formation of Preachers" 1.7.96, p. 209.

5. "Treatise on the Formation of Preachers" 4.17.193, p. 242.

Saint-Cher between the years 1240 to 1244.[6] Although a major part of the commentary makes for rather dull reading, certain passages in the work are composed with a clarity and force that remind one at times of the work of the modern French contemplative Simone Weil. In one such passage, our Dominican author notes that among the things "a man ought to see in contemplation," and ought "to write in the book of his heart," are "the needs of his neighbor":

> He ought to see [in contemplation] what he would like to have done for himself, if he were in such need, and how great is the weakness of every human being. . . . Understand from what you know about yourself the condition of your neighbor ["*Intellige ex te ipso quae sunt proximi tui*"]. And what you see in Christ and in the world and in your neighbor, write that in your heart.[7]

These lines are memorable for the compassionate attention they give to the neighbor in the context of contemplation. But I would like to think as well that their emphasis on true self-knowledge and their simple openness to Christ, to the neighbor, and to the world strike a distinctly Dominican note. The passage ends with a simple but impressive reference to the task of preaching. We are exhorted by our author first of all to understand ourselves, to be attentive to all that we see in the world around us and in our neighbor, and to reflect deep within our hearts on the things that we have observed.

6. See Robert E. Lerner, "Poverty, Preaching, and Eschatology in the Revelation Commentaries of Hugh of St Cher," in *The Bible in the Medieval World: Essays in Memory of Beryl Smalley*, ed. K. Walsh and D. Wood (Oxford: Blackwell, 1985), 157–189.

7. "Vidit Jacob," *Expositio Super Apocalypsim* chap. 1, ed. under the name of Thomas Aquinas, in *Opera Omnia, Opuscula Dubia* (Parma: Fiaccadori, 1868), 1:334–335. Translations from non-English texts, unless otherwise noted, are by the author.

But then we are told to go out and preach: "First see, then write, then send. . . . What is needed first is study, then reflection within the heart, and then preaching."[8]

What follows divides neatly into three sections:

1. Contemplation: A Vision of Christ
2. Contemplation: A Vision of the World
3. Contemplation: A Vision of the Neighbor

CONTEMPLATION: A VISION OF CHRIST

If you raise the subject of contemplation, for many people the first name that comes to mind is that of the Spanish Carmelite and mystic St. John of the Cross. But it is not the Carmelite John I want to talk about here. Instead, I would like to consider, for a moment, a much less-known spiritual author, a man whose name, by coincidence, was exactly the same as that of the celebrated Juan de la Cruz. But this other John, this less-known John of the Cross, this other spiritual author of the sixteenth century, was in fact a Dominican.[9]

By the time the Dominican Juan de la Cruz published his major work, the *Diálogo*, in the middle of the sixteenth century, the life of prayer or contemplation had come to be regarded, in many parts of Europe, as a rather daunting and highly specialized activity. There was a real risk, therefore, that a whole generation of people might begin to lose contact with the robust simplicity of the Gospel and

---

8. "Vidit Jacob," 1:334–335.

9. To appreciate the significance of the Dominican Juan de la Cruz in the history of spirituality, see the introduction by V. Beltrán de Heredia to a work by Juan de la Cruz entitled *Diálogo sobre la necesidad y provecho de la oración vocal*, published in *Biblioteca de Autores Cristianos* (Madrid: La Editorial Católica, 1962), 221:189–210. See also "Jean de la Croix, le Dominicain" by Simon Tugwell in *Mémoire Dominicaine* 2 (Spring 1993): 57–63. A translation of the *Diálogo* was expected to be in print by 1985 as part of the series called *Dominican Sources*. To my knowledge, however, this translation has not yet appeared.

might even cease to find encouragement in the teaching of Christ himself concerning prayer. What I find impressive about the work of Juan de la Cruz, the Dominican, is the way he exposed as exaggerated the emphasis in that period on the need for special interior experiences, and the way also in which he defended simple vocal prayer and underlined the importance in spiritual transformation of the ordinary, everyday struggle on the part of the Christian to live a life of virtue.

In his *Diálogo*, Juan de la Cruz was clearly determined to challenge those among his contemporaries who, in their writings, tended to exalt prayer almost beyond human reach, and who spoke of contemplation in a decidedly elitist and exclusive spirit. Accordingly, with the salt of the Gospel in his words—and with a kind of sharp humor—the Dominican asserted: "If indeed only contemplatives, in the strict sense of the word, can attain to heaven, then, as for myself, I would have to say what the Emperor Constantine replied to Bishop Acesius, who had shown himself to be extremely rigid at the Council of Nicaea: 'Take your ladder, and climb up to heaven by your own means if you're able' because the rest of us—we're nothing but sinners!"[10]

Behind the invective and sharp humor of Juan de la Cruz, there is an important statement being made. And it is this: Prayer or contemplation is not something that can be achieved by mere human effort, however well-intentioned or however strenuous. Prayer is a grace. It is a gift that lifts us beyond anything we ourselves could ever attain by ascetic practice or by meditative technique. Accordingly, communion with God, actual friendship with God in prayer, although impossible even for the strong, is something God

10. *Diálogo* 2.10.273, quoted in Tugwell, "Jean de la Croix, le Dominicain," 59.

himself can grant us in a second. "Sometimes," a thirteenth-century Dominican homily makes bold to declare, "a man is in a state of damnation before he begins his prayer and, before he is finished, he is in a state of salvation"![11] The preacher of this homily, William Peraldus, in answer to the question "Why everyone ought to be glad to learn how to pray," says something that we almost never hear stated three centuries later. For, by that time, as I have already indicated, prayer in its most authentic form was generally thought to be something very difficult to achieve. But Peraldus the Dominican states, without the least hesitation or self-consciousness, "Prayer is such an easy job!"[12]

This statement may, perhaps, sound naïve. But it draws its authority, I believe, from the Gospel itself. For is it not the case that in the Gospel, we are encouraged by Christ to pray with great simplicity of heart and straightforwardness? When, over the years, Dominicans have found themselves confronted with detailed methods and techniques of meditation, and with long lists of instructions on what to do and what not to do, their reaction has almost always been the same: they instinctively feel that something has gone wrong. The reaction of Bede Jarrett, the English Dominican, is typical. In one place he notes, with real regret, how on occasion prayer can become "reduced to hard and fast rules" and can be so "mapped-out" and "regimented" that "it hardly seems at all to be the language of the heart." When this happens, in the memorable words of Jarrett, "All adventure has gone, all the personal touches, and all the contemplation. We are too worried and harassed to think of God. The instructions are so detailed and insistent that we forget

11. William Peraldus, "Sermon on Prayer," in *Early Dominicans,* 168.
12. Peraldus, 167.

what we are trying to learn. As a consequence, we get bored and so no doubt does God."[13]

St. Teresa of Avila, writing on one occasion on the subject of prayer, makes quite a remarkable confession. She says that "some books on the subject of prayer" that she was reading encouraged her to set aside, as a positive hindrance, "the thought of Christ's humanity."[14] Teresa tried to follow this path for a while, but she soon realized that a prayer life that excluded Christ, although mystical in some way, was a path wholly mistaken. Illuminating, in this context, is the reaction of a Dominican theologian of the sixteenth century, Francisco de Vitoria, to any kind of abstract mysticism. Vitoria writes:

> There is a new kind of contemplation, which is practiced by the monks these days, consisting of meditating on God and the angels. They spend a long time in a state of elevation, thinking nothing. This is, no doubt, very good, but I do not find much about it in scripture, and it is, honestly, not what the saints recommend. Genuine contemplation is reading the bible and the study of true wisdom.[15]

That last statement from Vitoria betrays, if I am not mistaken, the direct influence of St. Dominic. Dominic never composed for his brethren any kind of devotional or spiritual text or testament. He was

13. See Bede Jarrett, "Contemplation," in *Meditations for Layfolk* (London: Catholic Truth Society, 1946), 182.
14. Teresa of Avila, *The Life of Saint Teresa of Avila by Herself*, trans. J.M. Cohen (London: Penguin, 1957), 153–157.
15. Francisco de Vitoria, *Commentarios a la Seconda Secondae de S. Tomas*, ed. V. Beltrán de Herédia (Salamanca: Biblioteca de Teólogos españoles, 1952), 6:2-2.182.4, quoted in Tugwell, "A Dominican Theology of Prayer," *Dominican Ashram* 1 (1982): 137.

a preacher first and last, not a writer. And yet, even at this distance in time, there are available to us within the tradition a surprising number of details concerning his way of prayer and contemplation. One reason for this is Dominic's own extraordinary temperament. He possessed an exuberance of nature that, far from being suppressed by the life of prayer and contemplation, seems in fact to have been wonderfully awakened and released. He was a man, as Cardinal Villot once remarked, "stupefyingly free."[16] At prayer in particular he could hardly, it seems, contain himself. Often, he would cry out to God at the top of his voice. As a result, even his private prayer was a kind of open book to his brethren. At night, when he was alone in the church, his voice would often be heard echoing throughout the entire convent.

So Dominic prays with all that he is—body and soul. He prays privately with intense and humble devotion. And, with that same deep faith and profound emotion, he prays in public the prayer of the Mass. Although the intensity of Dominic's faith and feeling may be unusual, as is the extraordinary length of his night vigils, for the rest his prayer seems indistinguishable from that of any ordinary devout Christian man or woman. His prayer is never in any way esoteric. It is always simple, always ecclesial.

One of the great merits, in my view, of the Dominican contemplative tradition is its dogged resistance to the esoteric aura or spiritual glamour that tends to surround the subject of contemplation. The well-known preacher in the English province Vincent McNabb, for example, with characteristic good humor, liked now and again to bring the subject of contemplation back down from the high clouds

16. Jean-Marie Villot, "Homelia in Basilica Sanctae Sabinae," *Analecta Sacri Ordinis Fratrum Praedicatorum* 39 (July–September 1970): 543.

of mysticism to the plain earth of Gospel truth. Concerning the question of prayer, for example, as presented in the parable of the Pharisee and the publican, McNabb writes:

> The Publican did not know he was justified. If you had asked him, "Can you pray?" he would have said, "No, I cannot pray. I was thinking of asking the Pharisee. He seems to know all about it. I could only say I was a sinner. My past is so dreadful. I cannot imagine myself praying. I am better at stealing."[17]

In *The Nine Ways of Prayer*, we are afforded a glimpse of St. Dominic himself repeating the publican's prayer while lying down prostrate on the ground before God. "His heart," we are told, "would be pricked with compunction, and he would blush at himself and say, sometimes loudly enough for it actually to be heard, the words from the Gospel, 'Lord, be merciful to me, a sinner.'"[18] Without exception I find that, in the prayer lives of the Dominican preachers I most admire, there is always something of that common neediness and that Gospel simplicity. When at prayer, these preachers are not afraid to speak to God directly, as to a friend. But always they return instinctively to the straightforward Gospel prayer of petition. Here is Aquinas, for example:

> I come before you as a sinner, O God, Source of all mercy. I am unclean, I beseech you to cleanse me. O Sun of Justice, give sight to a blind man. . . . O King of Kings, clothe one who is destitute.

17. Vincent McNabb, *The Craft of Prayer* (London: Burns & Oates, 1935), 77.
18. Quoted in "The Second Way of Prayer" of *The Nine Ways of Prayer of St. Dominic*, in *Early Dominicans*, 95.

Almighty, everlasting God, you see that I am coming to the sacrament of your only Son, our Lord Jesus Christ. I come to it as a sick man to the life-giving healer, as one unclean to the source of mercy . . . as one who is poor and destitute to the Lord of heaven and earth.[19]

The words of this prayer are prayed in deep poverty of spirit. But the prayer is said with utter confidence all the same. And why? Because the words of the prayer are Gospel words, and because Christ, the life-giving healer and source of mercy, is at its center.[20]

CONTEMPLATION: A VISION OF THE WORLD

In some religious traditions, the contemplative life implied an almost complete turning away from the world—in the case of certain ascetic religious, a rejection not only of their immediate family and friends but also of people in general, or at least those who appeared to be dominated by weakness or by worldly passion. Fortunately, however, the impulse toward contemplation in the lives of the best-known Dominican preachers and saints was never characterized by that sort of rigid, judgmental attitude. A good example, I think, of the Dominican approach is that short statement already quoted above by the anonymous Dominican friar writing at Saint-Jacques in Paris in the thirteenth century: "Among the things a man ought to see in contemplation," he wrote, "are the needs of his neighbor" and also "how great is the weakness of every human being." So the authentic

19. Thomas Aquinas, Prayers 1 and 2 of "Piae Preces," in *Opera Omnia, Opuscula Dubia* (Parma: Fiaccadori, 1869), 24:241–242.

20. For some further reflection on the place of Christ in early Dominican spirituality, see *Christ among the Early Dominicans: Representations of Christ in the Texts and Images of the Order of Preachers*, ed. Kent Emery, Jr. and Joseph P. Wawrykow (Notre Dame, IN: University of Notre Dame Press, 1998).

contemplative in our tradition, the authentic apostle, does not call down curses on the sinful world. But, instead, conscious of his or her own weakness, and humbly identified, therefore, with the world's need, the Dominican calls down a blessing.

In an unusually striking moment in *The Dialogue* of St. Catherine of Siena, the saint is asked by God the Father to lift up her eyes to him so that he might demonstrate, in some way, the extent of his passionate care for the whole world. "Look at my hand," the Father says to her. When Catherine does this, she sees at once—and the vision must have astonished her—the entire world being somehow held up and enclosed in God's hand. Then, the Father says to her, "My daughter, see now and know that no-one can be taken away from me. . . . They are mine. I created them and I love them ineffably. And so, in spite of their wickedness, I will be merciful to them . . . and I will grant what you have asked me with such love and sorrow."[21] What is immediately obvious from this account is that Catherine's passionate devotion to the world does not spring simply from the instinct of a generous heart. No—it is something grounded also in a profound theological vision and understanding. And this fact holds true for other Dominicans as well. The vision of Thomas Aquinas, for example, has been characterized by the German Thomist Josef Pieper as nothing less than a theologically founded "worldliness"![22]

21. Catherine of Siena, *The Dialogue* 18, trans. Suzanne Noffke (New York: Paulist, 1980), 56–57.

22. "It was as a theologian that Thomas cast his choice for the worldliness represented by the works of Aristotle. What is truly exciting about this choice is the reason Thomas gives for it. . . . In Aristotle's fundamental attitude toward the universe, in his affirmation of the concrete and sensuous reality of the world, Thomas recognized something entirely his own, belonging to himself as a Christian. . . . To put it in a nutshell, this element was the same as the Christian affirmation of Creation" (Josef Pieper, *Guide to Thomas Aquinas*, trans. Richard and Clara Winston [Notre Dame, IN: University of Notre Dame Press, 1962], 48–49).

Pieper's claim may at first surprise us. But, properly understood, a similar assertion can, I think, be made not only about Catherine's vision but also about the vision of Dominic himself.

My favorite image of St. Dominic is one painted on wood, which can be seen at the Church of Santa Maria della Mascarella in Bologna. It records "the miracle of bread," which, according to tradition, took place at the convent of Santa Maria della Mascarella. In this medieval work, Dominic's contemplative identity is indicated by the black capuce over his head. But the man we see before us is, first and last, *vir evangelicus*, a man of the Gospel *in persona Christi*, surrounded by his brethren and seated at a table, a meal, which as well as recalling "the miracle of bread" at once suggests a communal and liturgical life, a real Eucharistic fellowship. His look is one of extraordinary candor. And his physical presence gives the impression of a man of robust simplicity, a man entirely at ease with himself and with the world around him. In all of medieval iconography, I can think of no other religious painting or fresco in which a saint is shown, as here, looking out at the world with such serene confidence and ease of spirit.

One small detail worth noting is the way Dominic's right hand takes hold of the bread so decisively while his left hand, no less firm and strong, holds on to the table. The Dominic of this painting, like the Dominic of history, clearly possesses a very firm and very vital hold on the immediate world around him. The characterization of Dominic as "the saint of *interior* experience" (in contrast to Francis of Assisi, "the saint of nature") is accurate only from one limited point of view.[23] Dominic was a man unusually responsive to the world around him. A realist as much as a visionary, he stood out

23. See C. Pera, *La vita interiore di S. Domenico* (Florence: 1921), 66 (emphasis added).

among his contemporaries not only as a man of God but also as someone notably quick, flexible, and generous in his response to the immediate demands of his time.

That sense of openness to the world is a marked characteristic of many of the great Dominican preachers. "When I became a Christian," noted Lacordaire, "I did not lose sight of the world."[24] On one occasion, deliberately taking to task those religious people, some of them monks and priests, whose passion for the absolute tended to make them indifferent to the world and to "the true inwardness of things," to the fact that "things exist in themselves, with their own proper nature and needs,"[25] Yves Congar sought to highlight what he considered an important, if unexpected, lay quality in the Dominican vision of Aquinas. In Congar's opinion, someone who is "authentically lay,"[26] such as Aquinas, is "one for whom, through the very work which God has entrusted to him, the substance of things in themselves is real and interesting."[27] Congar strikes a similar note in a letter written to a fellow Dominican in 1959. Expressing a certain disinterest in what he referred to as "the distinction 'contemplative/ active life,'" Congar wrote:

> If my God is the God of the Bible, the living God, the "I am, I was, I am coming," then God is inseparable from the world and from human beings. . . . My action, then, consists in handing myself over to my God, who allows me to be the link for his divine

24. Jean-Baptiste Henri Lacordaire, *Le Testament* (*Notice sur le rétablissement en France de l'Ordre des Frères-Prêcheurs*), ed. C. de Montalembert (Paris: Douniol, 1870), 43.
25. Yves Congar, *Lay People in the Church: A Study for a Theology of the Laity*, trans. D. Attwater (London: Chapman, 1959), 17–18.
26. Congar, 21.
27. Congar, 17.

activity regarding the world and other people. My relationship to
God is not that of a cultic act, which rises up from me to Him,
but rather that of a faith by which I hand myself over to the action
of the living God, communicating himself according to his plan,
to the world and to other human beings. I can only place myself
faithfully before God and offer the fulness of my being and my
resources so that I can be there where God awaits me, the link
between this action of God and the world.[28]

Reading this extract from Congar's letter, I am immediately
reminded of one of the most remarkable visions of St. Catherine
of Siena. In it, St. Dominic appears precisely as a kind of "link"
between God's action and the world. Catherine reported to her
Dominican friend Fr. Bartolomeo that, first of all, she saw the Son
of God coming forth from the mouth of the Eternal Father. And,
then, to her amazement, she saw, emerging from the Father's breast,
"the most blessed Patriarch Dominic."[29] In order to "dispel her
amazement," the Father then said to her: "Just as this Son of mine,
by nature . . . spoke out before the world . . . so too Dominic, my
son by adoption."[30] The union between Dominic and the Father in
this vision could hardly be more intimate. But the preacher is not
seen here, in the usual mode of the contemplative, turning away
from the world toward God. Rather, with the Son of God, Dominic
is seen coming out from the One who, from the very beginning,
"so loved the world."

28. Yves Congar, "Action et contemplation: D'une lettre du père Congar au père Régamey
(1959)," *La Vie Spirituelle* 152, no. 727 (June 1998): 204.
29. See Raymond of Capua, *The Life of Catherine of Siena*, trans. C. Kearns (Wilmington,
DE: Glazier, 1980), 195.
30. *Life of Catherine of Siena*, 195.

In Congar's terms, Dominic's only action has been to surrender himself with faith and hope to the great, saving initiative of God. "There is only one thing that is real," Congar writes, "one thing that is true: to hand oneself over to God!"[31] But Congar is also well aware that, in the life of Dominic and the early friars, this handing over of self was never simply an individual act of will. It was always a surrender that involved, on the part of the brethren, a daily "following in the footsteps of their Savior"[32]—a radical and free acceptance, therefore, of an evangelical way of life.

It is here, at this point, that we meet head-on, as it were, some of the most obvious and most concrete forms of the contemplative dimension of the Dominican life: for example, choir in common, study, regular observance, the following of the Rule of St. Augustine, and the discipline of silence. These particular religious exercises and practices represented for St. Dominic a vital part of the evangelical way of life. But preaching remained paramount always. We can, I think, be grateful that, in recent decades, this message concerning preaching has come home to the Order loud and clear.

But what of the forms of regular and contemplative life that, ideally, should give support to preaching? Are we not, perhaps, today in need of recovering faith in this aspect of our tradition? Certainly, we are not monks; but neither are we a secular institute. Preaching is

31. Congar, "Action et contemplation," 204.
32. "The Early Dominican Constitutions," Second Distinction 31, in *Early Dominicans*, 467. For their chosen model of apostolic and contemplative life, the early Dominicans, while clearly influenced by certain forms of the monastic tradition, looked first and foremost to the life and example of Christ himself. Accordingly, with telling force, Aquinas notes in the *Summa theologiae* that "in order to teach preachers that they should not always be in the public gaze, Our Lord withdrew himself sometimes from the crowd" (*ST* 3.40.1 ad 3). Aquinas notes further that the life of the active preacher "built on an abundance of contemplation" was, in fact, "the life chosen by Christ" (*ST* 3.40.1 ad 2).

in itself, of course, a spiritual activity, even a contemplative one. But, for St. Dominic and the early friars, speaking about God (*de Deo*), which is the grace of preaching, presupposes first speaking with God (*cum Deo*), which is the grace of actual prayer or contemplation.[33] In the apostolic life adopted by the friars, the ecstasy of service or attention to the neighbor is unthinkable without the ecstasy of prayer or attention to God, and vice versa.

Obviously, in order to become a preacher, one does not have to be a monk of the desert or a master of mysticism or even a saint. But one does have to become, in Humbert of Romans' phrase, at least "a pray-er first."[34] One does have somehow to surrender oneself to God in prayer with at least the humble ecstasy of hope. "For," as we are reminded in *The Dialogue* of St. Catherine of Siena, "one cannot share what one does not have in oneself."[35]

In the end, of course, what matters is preaching. Christ did not say to us: "Be still and contemplate." He commanded us to go out

33. "The Early Dominican Constitutions," Second Distinction 31. The text reads: "like men of the Gospel, following in the footsteps of their Savior, talking either to God or about God, within themselves or with others" (*Early Dominicans*, 467).

34. Humbert is citing Augustine. He writes that the man who gets people to listen to him "should have no doubt that it is thanks to his devout prayers rather than to his well-trained fluency in speech. . . . So let him be a pray-er first, and then a teacher" ("Treatise on the Formation of Preachers" 4.19.233, in *Early Dominicans*, 252). While never overlooking the need for devoted prayer, Humbert openly acknowledges the fact that preaching can, like prayer itself, also be a form of holiness, "for the merit of preaching wins the gift of an increase of interior grace" (1.5.33, p. 195). Humbert even goes so far as to state: "Of all the spiritual exercises commonly practiced by spiritual men, those who have the grace for it ought to prefer the practice of preaching!" (4.21.260, p. 256).

35. Catherine of Siena, *Dialogue* 85, p. 157. In pursuit of the way of salvation, St. Dominic and other Dominicans after him, like St. Thomas, drew inspiration from ancient spiritual authors such as John Cassian. Concerning Dominic, Jordan of Saxony writes, "With the help of grace, this book [*Collationes Patrum*] brought him to . . . considerable enlightenment in contemplation and to a veritable peak of perfection" (*Jordan of Saxony: On the Beginnings of the Order of Preachers* 1.13, trans. Simon Tugwell [Dublin: Dominican, 1982], 3).

and preach (see Mark 16:15). Nevertheless, it is worth remembering here that, for the early friars, the grace of preaching, the surrender to God's living Word, was always intimately linked with a communal life of prayer and adoration, and with what Jordan of Saxony calls, in a fine phrase, "apostolic observance."[36]

The pattern of Dominican community life and community prayer was, in Jordan's understanding, not some sort of external or arbitrary discipline. Rather, Jordan saw it with enthusiasm as an opportunity for us to experience, here and now, in faith, Christ risen among us. In a letter he wrote to the brethren in Paris, Jordan speaks of the need for each one of us to hold fast to the bond of charity and keep faith with the brethren. If we should fail to do this, Jordan says, we risk an opportunity really to meet the risen Christ. For "the man" who cuts himself off from the unity of the brotherhood "may from time to time feel some very slight and fugitive consolation of spirit." But, in the opinion of Jordan, "he can never fully have sight of the Lord unless he is with the disciples gathered together in the house."[37]

In the practice of prayer, both public and private, and in the task of preaching, we discover, *in medio ecclesiae,* "in the midst of the Church," that Christ is now living his life within us. He is our risen brother to whom we can turn and speak as with a friend. "Consider," St. Thomas writes, quoting Chrysostom, "what a joy

36. The phrase occurs in a prayer addressed to St. Dominic, which may well have been composed, according to Vicaire, around the time of Dominic's canonization. See M.H. Vicaire, *Saint Dominic and His Times,* trans. K. Pond (Green Bay, WI: McGraw-Hill, 1964), 394, 530. The Latin is "apostolicae religioni," which Vicaire renders correctly as "l'observance apostolique."

37. Jordan of Saxony, "Letter to the Brethren at Paris," no. 56, in *Beati Iordani de Saxonia Epistulae,* ed. A. Walz, *MOFPH* 23 (Rome: Institutum Historicum Fratrum Praedicatorum, 1951), 69. See Jordan of Saxony, "Appendix: Other Letters," in *To Heaven with Diana! A Study of Jordan of Saxony and Diana d'Andalò with a Translation of the Letters of Jordan,* trans. Gerald Vann (Chicago: Collins, 1959), 157.

is granted you, what a glory is given you, to talk with God in your prayers, to converse with Christ, asking for whatever you want, whatever you desire."[38]

In contemplation, we turn our whole attention to God. But there is something else as well. God's Word, though utterly transcendent in its source, has come down into the world and has taken flesh. "God," as Simone Weil once remarked, "has to be on the side of the subject."[39] The initiative is always his. Accordingly, both in our work and in our prayer, we come to realize that Christ is not just the object of our regard. He is the Word alive within us, the friend "in whom we live and move and have our being." And thus, we can make bold to say, echoing the First Letter of St. John: this is contemplation—this is contemplative love—not so much that we contemplate God but that God has first contemplated us, and that now in us, in some sense, and even through us, as part of the mystery of his risen life in the Church, he contemplates the world.

More than fifty years ago, the French existentialist philosopher Albert Camus was invited to give a talk to a Dominican community in France at Latour-Maubourg. In his address, Camus strongly encouraged the brethren to maintain their own Dominican and Christian identity. "Dialogue is only possible," he remarked, "between people who remain what they are, and who speak the truth."[40] *Remain what you are.* It sounds like something fairly straightforward. But, as we know well, our identity as Dominicans, with its fundamental evangelical simplicity on the one hand and its great richness and variety of elements on the other, is something that can never

38. *ST* 2-2.83.2 ad 3.
39. Simone Weil, *The Notebooks*, trans. A. Wills (New York: Putnam, 1956), 2:358.
40. Albert Camus, "L'incroyant et les chretiens: Fragments d'une exposé fait au couvent des dominicains de Latour-Maubourg en 1948," in *Essais: Actuelles* (Paris: Gallimard, 1965), 1:372.

be taken for granted. In any given age, there is always the risk that some aspect of our identity will be lost or forgotten or ignored. And, as a result, the task of preaching—the main purpose of the Order—will suffer.

If there is one aspect or dimension of our life as Dominicans that, in this age, is vulnerable to neglect, it is—I have no doubt—the contemplative dimension. At the beginning of this talk, I recalled the story of an early Dominican who almost lost his faith through too much "contemplation." Now I very much doubt if that would happen in the Order today. Conditions may differ greatly from place to place. But, in this fast-speed, high-tech world, is it not the case that, as a generation, we are more likely to lose our faith through too much activity?

In this context, I find encouraging and challenging a comment made in a late interview by Marie-Dominique Chenu. Living at Saint-Jacques in Paris, in the same convent as the *frater anonymous* from the thirteenth century whom I quoted earlier, Chenu discovered that what he saw in the world somehow prompted him to contemplation. The world and the Word of God should not, Chenu insisted, be separated. "Our priority is to go out to the world. The world is the place where the Word of God takes on meaning."[41] This statement is one we understand today, being part of the inheritance that we have received from the twentieth century, and indeed from the thirteenth. But the comment from Chenu that I find most interesting concerns his own initial experience of the Order and the reason why he joined. "I had no intention of entering," he tells

---

41. M. Humbert Kennedy, "Interview with Marie-Dominique Chenu," *Dominican Ashram* 5, no. 2 (June 1986): 61.

us, "but I was impressed by the atmosphere of the place."[42] It was not, strictly speaking, a monastic atmosphere, Chenu recalls, but one of contemplation all the same. And it was "the contemplative atmosphere" that drew him. The brothers' devotion to study and the general air of intense and ascetic dedication remained with Chenu for many years. "All through my life," he said, "I have reaped the benefits of that contemplative cadre."[43]

The contemplative life itself, of course, receives attention from Aquinas in the *Summa theologiae*. You remember I spoke earlier in this section of the "lay spirit" in Aquinas—how he looked at the things of this world with respect. But, in the *Summa*, when he discusses the contemplative life, Aquinas emphasizes the importance of giving attention also to what he calls "eternal things." He writes, "The contemplative life consists in a certain liberty of spirit. Thus, Gregory says that *the contemplative life produces a certain freedom of mind, because it considers eternal things.*"[44]

That "freedom of mind," which comes from contemplation, is not something reserved only for enclosed contemplatives. Preachers, in fact, need that freedom perhaps more than anyone. For without it, they risk becoming prisoners of the spirit and fashions of the age. And what they preach, in the end, will not be the Word of God, but instead some word or some ideology of their own. And *that* word, *that* message, will be of little use to the world, even if preachers appear to be carrying it to the furthest frontiers of human need. For really to "come out into the open," preachers must first of all, as the Gospel reminds us, make a journey *within*. "God," Eckhart

42. Kennedy, 59.
43. Kennedy, 59.
44. *ST* 2-2.182.1 ad 2, trans. J. Aumann in Blackfriars Edition, vol. 46 (New York: Blackfriars/McGraw-Hill, 1966), 71.

says, "is in, we are out. God is at home, we are abroad. . . . God leads the just through narrow paths to the highway that they may come out into the open."[45]

CONTEMPLATION: A VISION OF THE NEIGHBOR

In traditional religious literature, the word "ecstasy" is often linked with that of contemplation. But nowadays, on the street, the word means one thing and one thing only: a very potent and very dangerous drug! Over the centuries, Dominicans have not been shy to use the word on occasion when talking about prayer or contemplation. But the following rather sharp and challenging comment from Eckhart on the subject is typical. He says, "If a man were in an ecstasy, as Saint Paul was, and knew that some sick man needed him to give him a bit of soup, I should think it far better if you would abandon your ecstasy out of love and show greater love in caring for the other in his need."[46] "Love": there it is, that small Gospel word, that harbinger of the grace of attention, that reminder to all of us of what contemplation—Christian contemplation—really means!

One of the statements about St. Dominic most often quoted is that he gave "the day to his neighbors, and the night to God."[47] It is a telling statement but, in a way, not strictly true. For, even after the day was over, in the great silence and solitude of Dominic's long night vigils, the neighbor was not forgotten. According to one of the

45. Meister Eckhart, "Sermon Sixty Nine," in *Meister Eckhart: German Sermons and Treatises*, ed. M.O'C. Walshe (London: Watkins, 1981), 2:169. It's worth noting that Eckhart's splendid phrase "come out into the open" was also used by Humbert of Romans in his "Treatise on the Formation of Preachers" 4.17.193.

46. Meister Eckhart, "Counsels on Discernment" 10, in *Meister Eckhart: The Essential Sermons*, trans. E. Colledge and B. McGinn (New York: Paulist, 1981), 258.

47. Jordan of Saxony, *Libellus de Principiis Ordinis Praedicatorum* 105, in *Monumenta Historica Sancti Patris Nostri Dominici,* Fasc. 2, *MOFPH* 16 (Rome: Institutum Historicum Fratrum Praedicatorum, 1933), 75.

saint's contemporaries—Brother John of Bologna—Dominic, after lengthy prayers, lying face down on the pavement of the church, would rise up and perform two simple acts of homage. First, within the church, he would "*visit* each altar in turn . . . until midnight." But then "he would go very quietly and *visit* the sleeping brethren; and, if necessary, he would cover them up."[48]

The way this account has been written down, one has the sense that Dominic's reverence for the individual altars in the church is somehow intimately related to his reverence and care for the sleeping brethren. It is almost as if Dominic is acknowledging, first of all, the presence of the sacred in the altars, and then—with no less reverence—that same presence in his own brethren. I have always been struck by a phrase that Yves Congar quoted many years ago from Nicholas Cabasilas. It reads, "Among all visible creatures, human nature alone can truly be an altar."[49] Congar himself, in his book *The Mystery of the Temple*, makes bold to say, "Every Christian is entitled to the name of 'saint' and the title of 'temple.'"[50] And again, echoing that same Pauline vision, Jordan of Saxony, the first Master of the Order after Dominic, wrote to a Dominican community of nuns, "The temple of God is holy, and you are that temple; nor is there any doubt but that the Lord is in his holy temple, dwelling within you."[51]

Among all those within the Dominican tradition who have spoken and written concerning the neighbor in contemplation, the

48. John of Bologna, "De Beato Dominico" 17, in *Vitae Fratrum*, 79. Emphasis added.

49. Quoted in Yves Congar, *The Mystery of the Temple*, trans. R.F. Trevett (Westminster, MD: Newman, 1962), 203.

50. Congar, 203.

51. Jordan of Saxony, "Letter to the Dominican Sisters at Bologna," no. 24, in *Beati Iordani de Saxonia Epistulae*, 28. See Jordan of Saxony, "Letter 11," in *To Heaven With Diana*, 79.

most outstanding in my view is St. Catherine of Siena. On the very first page of her *Dialogue*, we are told that "when she was at prayer, lifted high in spirit," God revealed to her something of the mystery and dignity of every human being. "Open your mind's eye," God said to her, "and you will see the dignity and beauty of my reasoning creature."[52] When Catherine opened her mind in prayer, she discovered not only a vision of God and a vision of herself in God as his image, but also a new and compassionate vision and understanding of her neighbor. "She immediately feels compelled," Catherine writes, "to love her neighbor as herself for she sees how supremely she herself is loved by God, beholding herself in the wellspring of the sea of the divine essence."[53]

Contained in these few words of Catherine there is, I believe, a profound yet simple truth: the source of her vision of the neighbor and the cause of her deep respect for the individual person is her contemplative experience. What Catherine receives in prayer and contemplation is what Dominic had received before her—not simply the command from God to love her neighbor as she had been loved, but an unforgettable insight beyond or beneath the symptoms of human distress, a glimpse into the hidden grace and dignity of each person. So deeply affected was Catherine by this vision of the neighbor that she remarked on one occasion to Raymond of Capua that if he could only see this beauty—the inner, hidden beauty—of the individual person as she saw it, he would be willing to suffer and die for it. "Oh Father . . . if you were to see the beauty of the human soul, I am convinced that you would willingly suffer death

---

52. Catherine of Siena, *Dialogue* 1, 25–26.
53. Catherine of Siena, "Letter to Raymond of Capua," no. 226, in *Le Lettere di S. Caterina da Siena*, ed. N. Tommasèo (Siena: Giuntini Bentivoglio, 1922), 3:297.

a hundred times, were it possible, in order to bring a single soul to salvation. Nothing in this world of sense around us can possibly compare in loveliness with a human soul."[54]

The assertion of a willingness to die a hundred times for the sake of the neighbor sounds extreme. But it is typical of Catherine. In another place, she writes, "Here I am, poor wretch, living in my body, yet in desire constantly outside my body! *Oimè! good gentle Jesus! I am dying and cannot die!*"[55] That last phrase, "I am dying and cannot die," Catherine repeats a number of times in her letters. Two centuries later, the Carmelite mystic St. Teresa of Avila also uses the same phrase, but in a very different way from Catherine. True to her Carmelite vocation, Teresa's whole attention is fixed with deep longing on Christ her Spouse. Without him, the world holds little or no interest. And so, in one of her poems, Teresa tells us that she is "dying" of great spiritual pain—because she cannot "die" physically as yet and be one with Christ in heaven:

> Straining to leave this life of woe,
> With anguish sharp and deep I cry:
> "*I die because I do not die.*"[56]

When Catherine uses the phrase "I die because I cannot die," she never uses it to express a desire to be out of this world. Of course,

54. Raymond of Capua, *Life of Catherine of Siena*, 146.

55. Catherine of Siena, "Letter to Raymond of Capua," no. 211, in *Le Lettere*, 3:225. See *The Letters of Catherine of Siena*, trans. Suzanne Noffke (Tempe, AZ: Arizona Center for Medieval and Renaissance Studies, 2001), 2:169.

56. Teresa of Avila, "Poem – 1," in *The Complete Works of St. Teresa of Avila*, ed. Allison Peers (London: Sheed & Ward, 1950), 3:278. Needless to say, the rather sharp contrast indicated here between Teresa and Catherine in no way reflects the full stature and great humanity of the Carmelite.

like Teresa, Catherine longs to be with Christ. But her passion for Christ compels her, as a Dominican, to want to serve the Body of Christ, the Church, here and now in the world, and in any way she can. Her anguish of longing comes from her awareness that all her efforts are inevitably limited. She writes, "*I am dying and cannot die! I am bursting and cannot burst because of my desire for the renewal of holy Church, for God's honor, and for everyone's salvation.*"[57]

The mysticism of Catherine of Siena, like that of Dominic, is an ecclesial mysticism. It is a mysticism of service, not a mysticism of psychological enthusiasm. God is, of course, for both Catherine and Dominic, always the primary focus of attention, but the neighbor and the neighbor's need are never forgotten. When, on one occasion, a group of hermits refused to abandon their solitary life in the woods even though their presence was badly needed by the Church in Rome, Catherine wrote at once to them with biting sarcasm. In one letter, she exclaimed, "Now really, the spiritual life is quite too lightly held if it is lost by change of place. Apparently, God is an acceptor of places, and is found only in a wood, and not elsewhere in time of need!"[58]

This outburst from Catherine does not mean that she had no appreciation for the ordinary aids and supports necessary for the contemplative life: for example, solitude, recollection, and silence. Silence, in particular, Catherine respected. But what she in no way approved of was the cowardly silence of certain ministers of the Gospel who, in her opinion, ought to have been crying out loud and

---

57. Noffke, *Letters of Catherine of Siena*, 2:169.
58. Catherine of Siena, "Letter 328 to Brother Antonio of Nizza of the Hermit Brothers of St. Augustine," in *Le Lettere di S. Caterina da Siena*, ed. N. Tommaseo (Siena: Giuntini Bentivoglio, 1940), 5:81.81. See *Saint Catherine of Siena as Seen in Her Letters*, ed. V.D. Scudder (London: J.M. Dent, 1927), 315.

clear on behalf of truth and justice. "Cry out as if you had a million voices," she urged. "It is silence which kills the world."[59]

Two centuries later, in a letter sent home to Spain by the Dominican preacher Bartolomé de Las Casas, we hear the same note of urgency. The year was 1545. Already, with no small courage, Bartolomé had discerned that his vocation was to become a voice for those who had no voice. Being confronted daily by the appalling degradation and torture of innocent people all around him, he was determined to keep silent no longer. "I believe," he wrote, "God wants me to fill heaven and earth, and the whole earth anew, with cries, tears and groans."[60]

Las Casas did not base the strength of his challenge on mere emotion. Again and again, we find the Dominican preacher appealing in his writings to what he called the "intelligence of the faith." According to Las Casas, the best way to arrive at Gospel truth was "by commending oneself earnestly to God, and by piercing very deeply—until one finds the foundations."[61] It was at this level of humble yet persistent meditation that Bartolomé encountered not just the truth about God, but God himself, the God of the Bible, the Father of Christ Jesus, the living God who, in Bartolomé's own words, has "a very fresh and living memory of the smallest and most forgotten."[62]

59. Catherine of Siena, "Letter 16," in *Le Lettere di S. Caterina da Siena*, ed. N. Tommaseo (Siena: Giuntini Bentivoglio, 1940), 1:55. See Mary Ann Fatula, *Catherine of Siena's Way* (London: Darton, Longman & Todd, 1987), 72.

60. Quoted in Guy Bedouelle, *In the Image of St. Dominic: Nine Portraits of Dominican Life* (San Francisco: Ignatius, 1994), 99.

61. Bartolomé de Las Casas, *Confessionario*, 1552, O.E. 5:239b, quoted in Gustavo Gutiérrez, *Las Casas: In Search of the Poor of Christ* (New York: Orbis Books, 1993), 15.

62. Bartolomé de Las Casas, *Carta al Consejo*, 1531, O.E. 5:44b, quoted in Gutiérrez, 61.

By allowing himself to be exposed in this way to the face of Christ crucified in the afflicted, Bartolomé was a true son of his father Dominic. For Dominic was a man possessed not only by a vision of God but also by a profound inner conviction of people's need. And it was to the men and women of his own time, to his own contemporaries, whose need he received almost like a wound in prayer, that Dominic was concerned to communicate all that he had learned in contemplation.

At the very core of St. Dominic's life, there was a profound contemplative love of God—that first and last. But reading through the very early accounts of Dominic's prayer life, what also immediately impresses is the place that is accorded to others—to the afflicted and oppressed—within the act of contemplation itself. The *alii*—the others—are not simply the passive recipients of Dominic's graced preaching. Even before the actual moment of preaching, when St. Dominic becomes a kind of channel of grace, these people—the afflicted and oppressed—inhabit "the inmost shrine of his compassion." They form part of the *"contemplata"* in *contemplata aliis tradere*. Jordan of Saxony writes:

> God had given [Dominic] a special grace to weep for sinners and for the afflicted and oppressed; he bore their distress in the inmost shrine of his compassion, and the warm sympathy he felt for them in his heart spilled over in the tears which flowed from his eyes.[63]

In part, of course, this means simply that when he prays, Dominic remembers to intercede for those people he knows to be in

---

63. Jordan of Saxony, *Libellus de Principiis Ordinis Praedicatorum* 12, p. 32. See Tugwell, *Jordan of Saxony: On the Beginnings of the Order of Preachers* 1.12, p. 3.

need, and for sinners especially. But there is something more—some "special grace," to use Jordan's phrase. The wound of knowledge that opens up Dominic's mind and heart in contemplation, allowing him with an awesome unprotectedness to experience his neighbor's pain and need, cannot be accounted for simply by certain crowding memories of pain observed or by his own natural sympathy. The apostolic wound Dominic receives, which enables him to act and to preach, is a contemplative wound.

CHAPTER TWO

What Makes for Good Preaching?[1]

In *Evangelii Gaudium*, when Pope Francis talks about the homily, he reminds us that, in practice, it should not only be "a consoling encounter with God's Word, a constant source of renewal and growth," but also "an intense and happy experience of the spirit."[2] *An intense and happy experience.* That preaching can, on occasion, be indeed as wonderful as that, I have no doubt. But I also know that if today the people of God, our contemporaries, were consulted on the question, whether here in Italy or in Ireland or in the United States, and were asked for their impressions of Sunday homilies, the words "intense" and "happy" would not be the first adjectives to spring to their minds! All of us, as Pope Francis acknowledges in the same passage, "suffer because of homilies: the laity from having to listen to them, and the clergy from having to preach them!"[3]

Several years ago, I read a statement on the subject of preaching that surprised and saddened me. It appeared in a short article titled "The Pastor with the Empty Soul." The author, a North American

1. A talk given originally to the International Colloquium on *Dei Verbum* at the Angelicum (Rome, February 27, 2016).
2. Francis, *Evangelii Gaudium* 135, apostolic exhortation, November 24, 2013, vatican.va.
3. *Evangelii Gaudium* 135. An impressive number of paragraphs in *Evangelii Gaudium* are devoted to the homily. See nos. 135–175. The post-synodal apostolic exhortation of Pope Benedict XVI on the Word of God, *Verbum Domini*, offers a helpful reflection on the homily in the context of the sacred liturgy (see nos. 52–59).

parish priest, claimed that some of his fellow priests stand up "week after week . . . in front of their congregations, and proclaim the Gospel message, not with passion and conviction but from the hollowness of their empty soul." Then, he said, and the phrase is terrible, "They are burned out without ever having been on fire."[4] The priest, the author of this particular article, didn't offer any solution to the problem. But one word in his reflections can, I would suggest, serve as a pointer to the solution. It is the word "fire." Of St. Dominic we read in the ninth of the *Nine Ways of Prayer* that "in his meditation a fire was enkindled."[5] *In his meditation.* The fire, the urgency, the fervor of Dominic's preaching had its source in his practice of prayer. It was in prayer, we are told in the same text, that Dominic attained to "the fullness of sacred scripture and the very heart of the understanding of God's words, and also a power and courage to preach the gospel with fervor that nothing could intimidate, and also a hidden intimacy with the Holy Spirit to know hidden mysteries."[6]

In a homily, what matters first and last is that the Word of God is not only preached but *heard.* For that to happen, however, the preacher must have not only some knowledge of the needs of the people he is addressing, but also intimate knowledge of the message he has been called to preach. And that task, of course, demands preparation. Is theology part of that preparation? I raise the question here because, surprisingly, very little reference is made to theology in the recent ecclesial documents on preaching. That said, however, the *Homiletic Directory* produced in 2015 by the Congregation

4. *The Priest* 51 (September 1995): 9.
5. *The Nine Ways of Prayer of Saint Dominic,* ed. and trans. Simon Tugwell (Dublin: Dominican, 1978), 46.
6. *Nine Ways of Prayer,* 46.

for Divine Worship does acknowledge at one point that it is "very appropriate" for a given preacher "to share the fruits of scholarship."[7] Also, in a document produced by the United States Conference of Catholic Bishops entitled *Preaching the Mystery of Faith: The Sunday Homily*, there is included one clear, encouraging statement. It reads, "Preachers should have the *habitus* of theology: the steady practice of reading the theological masters (both ancient and modern) and meditating on the great questions that they entertain."[8] In *Evangelii Gaudium*, Pope Francis makes a brief, passing reference to "the charism of the theologians." The particular concern he expresses is that "scholarly efforts" should not take the form of mere "desk-bound theology," but rather lead directly to the work of evangelization.[9]

The homily, given its liturgical context, is a phenomenon altogether different from an academic lecture, a talk delivered in a university classroom. That's why there is no need whatsoever for generic or abstract reflections in a homily. Such adventures of thought, however interesting in themselves, are more likely to obscure than reveal the power and simplicity of the Gospel message. But the act of preaching differs from the preparation that precedes it. And part of that preparation, if wise, will involve thinking—hard thinking— about the particular Gospel text. And such thinking, such pondering on the meaning of the Gospel passage, will inevitably draw much of its energy of enquiry, and its sheer delight in understanding, from the wisdom of theology.

---

7. Congregation of Divine Worship and the Discipline of the Sacraments, *Homiletic Directory* 7, June 29, 2014, vatican.va.

8. United States Conference of Catholic Bishops, *Preaching the Mystery of Faith: The Sunday Homily* (Washington, DC: USCCB, 2013), 35.

9. *Evangelii Gaudium* 133.

In the Dominican tradition, study of this kind, theology of this kind, is not something completely distinct from *lectio divina*. On the contrary, it is understood to form part of the contemplative quest, and can even be said, in the opinion of Aquinas, to assume the *modus orativus*.[10] Study can become, in other words, an *active* form of prayer. The preacher, seriously reflecting on the Gospel, chooses instinctively not to remain at a safe, academic distance. In attitude and in spirit, he is a man on his knees before the mystery; he is the servant, not the master of the Word. Accordingly, all the reflections he undertakes—the research, the questioning of the text, etc.—have their source not in pride or mere cleverness, but rather in profound reverence for the Word and in a humble desire for wisdom. That, if not already the reality, should be the aim, the ideal.

What consequences follow if no preparation for preaching the Gospel takes place, if the Sunday homily, for example, is not preceded by a close, attentive reading of the relevant texts and prayerful study? Well, one unhappy consequence is that the priest or the deacon, instead of preaching God's Word, will almost inevitably fall back on a soap box of his own ideas, twisting the readings to fit in with predictable, half-baked opinions and partisan dogma. As a result, instead of the Gospel vision, instead of the Good News, we have dull moralism and ideology.

The Word of God comes to us "full of grace and truth" (John 1:14). But that fullness will be badly served if individual ministers of the Gospel decide to be preachers of truth only or of grace only. Once that happens, once preaching is no longer based on the full

10. Thomas Aquinas, *Scriptum super libros Sententiarum* 1, prologue, a. 5, cited in J.-P. Torrell, *Saint Thomas Aquinas*, vol. 2, *Spiritual Master*, trans. Robert Royal (Washington, DC: The Catholic University of America Press, 2003), 17.

Gospel message, the Word becomes, in a sense, fractured. We will have, on the one hand, proponents of a false rigorism, hard-line and hard-nosed messengers of a one-sided truth, and, on the other hand, messengers no less extreme and no less numerous but, this time, proponents of what might be called cheap or easy grace, priests and deacons addicted to superficial, cheery affirmations.

What is needed, both in the life of prayer and in the task of preaching, is the fullness of grace and truth. We need truth so that we may not be able "to hide from God," as St. Bernard of Clairvaux puts it, and we need grace so that we may not "wish to hide."[11] Truth without grace in the hands of the preacher today would be something truly terrifying, a harsh, fundamentalist weapon. But grace without truth would be a Santa Claus illusion, a mere sentimentality.

In this context, I am struck by a passage in the autobiographical work *Donum et Mysterium* by Pope John Paul II: "The minister of the Word," he wrote, "must possess and pass on that knowledge of God which is not a mere deposit of doctrinal truths but a personal and living experience of the Mystery."[12] The statement is strong and memorable, but also challenging. It alerts us to the fact that only the individual whose life has been marked in some way by a personal faith encounter with Christ Jesus, and by the radiant, glad surprise, therefore, of redeeming love, can dare to preach the Gospel. Possessing knowledge *about* Christ, having accurate, orthodox information, is one thing. But to know him intimately in living faith, to know him as one's redeemer in the depth of one's soul, is something else. "What is essential," we are reminded in *Evangelii Gaudium*, "is that

11. Bernard of Clairvaux, Sermon 74:8, in *Sermons on the Song of Songs*, trans. I.M. Edmonds (Kalamazoo, MI: Cistercian, 1980), 4:92–93.

12. John Paul II, *Gift and Mystery: On the 50th Anniversary of My Priestly Ordination* (New York: Image Books, 1996), 111.

the preacher be certain that God loves him, that Jesus Christ has saved him and that his love always has the last word."[13]

But what are we to say, in this context, about "the deposit of doctrinal truths"? In the task of evangelization, how important today is doctrinal preaching? For most of our contemporaries, the word "doctrine," I suspect, conjures up a world remote from the immediacy of everyday experience. As a result, the preacher, in order to appear relevant, may well be tempted to avoid drawing directly or indirectly from "the deposit of doctrinal truths." And that would be an enormous pity. I say this because, properly understood, doctrine is nothing other than the articulation in theological terms of the great mystery of God and of the stupendous realities of creation, Incarnation, and redemption. It is, therefore, the very lifeblood of evangelization. Far from being something preachers should avoid in homilies, these key doctrinal themes, properly understood and preached with conviction and joy, are Good News incarnate.

That said, doctrine should obviously not be presented in a homily as it would be for an academic audience or for students in a theology classroom. When a homily is good, the focus of attention will go, first and last, to Christ present in the Scripture readings for that particular day. Critical questions, however, that touch on the deepest truths of the faith (on the mystery of Christ's humanity and divinity, for example) will quite often be evoked by the readings themselves, and at that point, doctrine can be an enormous help and guide for the homilist.

Often, as their primary means of communication, the inspired authors of the Old and New Testaments make use of parable and story. And that is not surprising. Particularly strong and vivid

13. *Evangelii Gaudium* 151.

images will almost always impact the reader or the listener with greater immediacy than abstract ideas. It's not hard, therefore, to understand why in the Scriptures God speaks to us more like a poet than an academic theologian, and why it could be said that by far the most memorable expression of Christ's teaching is in the form of parables. From this bright, imaginative example of Christ, the preacher today has everything to learn. Of course, not many of the chosen ministers of the Word are poets. But all of us, surely, at one time or another, have been privileged to come to know or to witness, whether through reading or through experience, what might be called "enacted parables" in the lives of God's people. And these hidden stories of courage and self-sacrifice, these small or great events of grace, all of them happening in the complicated world we know so well, can be shared by the preacher in his homily in order to awaken new desire for God and new hope for the coming of God's kingdom.

The core event, the great story celebrated at every Eucharist, is the drama of the death and Resurrection of Christ Jesus. It is a story of wondrous compassion, an event that is not only recalled but also made wonderfully present through the Scripture readings and through the sacrament itself. Given this fact, one key task of the preacher will be to make lively the link between the event of grace, as celebrated in the liturgy, and the reality of that same grace as already experienced—at least in some measure—in the events of daily life: Christ the Lord alive and risen in the lives and hearts of his people. Ideally, therefore, the homily at every Mass will be a joyous recognition of the Paschal Mystery, its core message focused, at least implicitly, on the drama of divine mercy about to be enacted in the sacrament, and also on the drama of that same mercy manifest daily in the lives of believers.

It goes without saying that the homily, for any given parish, for any local assembly, is of great importance. Nevertheless, when it comes to the task of preaching in general, an exclusive focus on the homily might very easily make us forget that evangelization is not, in the first place, about the faithful in the parish and their immediate needs, but rather about the needs of those in the world who, as yet, do not know Christ, or who may have rejected Christ for one reason or another, or who have never felt drawn to the Gospel. Those called to the task of evangelization include, of course, not merely priests and deacons, but all the members of God's people in virtue of Baptism, men and women alike. "Every Christian," we are reminded in *Evangelii Gaudium,* "is challenged, here and now, to be actively engaged in evangelization; indeed, anyone who has truly experienced God's saving love does not need much time or lengthy training to go out and proclaim that love."[14]

Preaching today is often spoken of in the context of what's called "the New Evangelization." What this refers to is not the search for a new gospel; it refers rather to the urgent need for us to discover, in a world so dramatically changed, new ways to preach the Good News. This challenge is one that confronts every generation of believers and every generation of preachers. In our own times, a key part of any effective preaching of the Gospel will involve, of necessity, making use of the new methods and means available to

---

14. *Evangelii Gaudium* 120. In similar vein, we read in *Christifideles Laici*: "The lay faithful, precisely because they are members of the Church, have the vocation and mission of proclaiming the Gospel: they are prepared for this work by the sacraments of Christian initiation and by the gifts of the Holy Spirit" (John Paul II, *Christifidelis Laici* 33, encyclical letter, December 30, 1988, vatican.va). See also Thomas Aquinas, *ST* 3.72.5 ad 2.

us for evangelization. What dominates culture nowadays, especially where communication is concerned, is the internet, but also of course all the other new forms of social media. These powerful advances in technology can have a decidedly positive impact on society but also, it has to be admitted, a negative impact as well. Nevertheless, the new technology really does offer the preacher today a fresh and exciting means of communicating the Gospel to a new generation.

Many centuries ago, the Dominicans set themselves to preach not only inside churches but also outside in the streets of the towns and thoroughfares they visited. Today, communicating the Gospel by making use of the internet and social media could be described as a twenty-first-century way of "preaching in the streets." It is certainly a way of going out to where people, especially young people, are most likely to be engaged at the level of ideas and vision, and where they are most likely to listen.

Among our contemporaries in the Church, the preacher who has, to my knowledge, best seized the opportunity offered by the explosion taking place in the world of technology and new media is Bishop Robert Barron of the Diocese of Winona-Rochester. Barron has been called, and for good reason, "the internet's parish priest." His ministry is called Word on Fire. Those being reached by the ministry in recent times number not hundreds but millions of men and women—believers, atheists, agnostics, people of all ages and from almost every nation on earth. Naturally, Barron is concerned that those who are ministers of the Gospel make efficient and imaginative use of the new technology. But he is even more concerned that all preachers today be grounded in what he calls "the old technology of books"[15]; grounded, in other words, in the theological and spiritual tradition of the Church and having, as a result, something to say that's really worth saying. Merely being in possession of a certain flair for using social media will never, by itself, add up to effective evangelization.

One of the greatest challenges facing evangelization today, at least in the West, is the marked indifference to religion evident in so many of our contemporaries. It's almost as if, with regard to the Christian religion in particular, our contemporaries are color-blind or tone-deaf. How, then, can they be made aware of the sheer depth and range, the unmatched truth and radiance of Christian belief? How can words of preachers today—words both new *and* ancient—touch the imaginations of our contemporaries? It's obvious that the task of the New Evangelization will require ideas specific to the challenge of our own times. Nevertheless, the core answer, the beginning answer, will be the same today as it has always been. And that is to look to the life of Christ Jesus, the preacher, and to the lives of saints and preachers such as Dominic and Catherine.

What strikes one immediately about men and women shaped by the Gospel vision is that all the words they speak are at one with the lives they lead. Catherine of Siena, on the subject of preaching, gave this advice to Raymond of Capua: "Learn from the Master of truth, who preached virtue only *after* he had practiced it."[16] Clearly, above all else, what gives authority to the words of the preacher is integrity of life. No style of utterance, no special technique in speaking, will ever be able to match that grace, that authority. Accordingly,

15. See Robert Barron with Brandon Vogt, "Father Barron's Seven Tips for New Evangelization," *Our Sunday Visitor*, December 30, 2012, 16.

16. Catherine of Siena, "Letter 226," in *The Letters of Catherine of Siena*, trans. Suzanne Noffke (Tempe, AZ: Arizona Center for Medieval and Renaissance Studies, 2001), 2:5.

ministers of the Word today, being aware of their own limitations and of the gap between their words and their lives, will be continually asking God for the grace of a deeper conversion, a life of greater integrity.

It is no easy task to evangelize in the pluralistic society of the present age. Increasingly, the Catholic vision finds itself opposed by the dominant powers of secularism, individualism, and relativism. How best, then, to respond? One temptation would be to yield to the pressure and, for the sake of short-term popularity, ignore the challenging demands of the Gospel. Another temptation, no less sad and unenlightened, would be to adopt, with regard to the world, a fortress mentality, employing for the most part the language of condemnation. Should that occur, instead of the Good News being communicated, almost the only news the world would hear would be a certain number of predictable pronouncements on issues such as contraception, the ordination of women, and abortion. Pope Benedict XVI, in an impressive talk he gave to a group of bishops in 2006, referred to the contemporary discussion in the media surrounding these issues. After noting how often and how insistently all three are raised by journalists, he remarked: "If we let ourselves be drawn into these discussions, the Church is then identified with certain commandments or prohibitions; we give the impression that we are moralists with a few somewhat antiquated convictions, and not even a hint of the true greatness of the faith appears."[17]

For evangelization today, there is one superb example given to us in the account by St. Luke of the risen Lord's post-Resurrection appearance at Emmaus. Before Jesus preaches, before attempting to

17. Benedict XVI, "Conclusion of the Meeting of the Holy Father with the Bishops of Switzerland," November 9, 2006, vatican.va.

speak in depth to the two confused disciples, he *listens* to what they have to say. He even goes to the trouble of asking them about their experience. And, in order to keep the conversation alive, he walks with them in the *wrong* direction, as it were, toward Emmaus, not Jerusalem. Preaching today, if it is going to be effective, demands that we do a lot of listening. It demands that we are prepared to walk with people who may have views very different from our own. This openness of spirit, this instinct for dialogue, is of course part of the Dominican tradition at its ordinary best. Aquinas tells us:

> When taking up or rejecting opinions, a person should not be led by love or hate concerning who said them but rather by the certainty of truth. He [Aristotle] says we should love both kinds of people: those whose opinions we follow, and those whose opinions we reject. For both study to find the truth and, in this way, both give us assistance.[18]

The Dominican martyr-bishop Pierre Claverie, our great contemporary, makes this point even more forcibly. He writes, "I have need of the truth of the other. I not only accept the other is a distinct subject with freedom of conscience, but I accept that he or she may possess a part of the truth I don't have without which my own search for truth cannot be realized."[19] This does not mean, of course, that I must somehow abandon my own fundamental beliefs in order to engage in authentic dialogue with a person of a different religion

18. Thomas Aquinas, *Sententia super metaphysicam* 12.9.2566 (Torino: Marietti, 1971), 599. Elsewhere Thomas notes that "any truth no matter by whom it is said is from the Holy Spirit [*omne verum, a quocumque dicatur, est a Spiritu Sancto*]" (*ST* 1-2.109.1 ad 1).

19. Quoted in Jean-Jacque Pérennès, *A Life Poured Out: Pierre Claverie of Algeria* (New York: Orbis Books, 2007), 148.

or of no religion. No, that would be sheer naïveté and the opposite of dialogue. What it does mean, however, is that sometimes, really encountering a person of a different religion can have the effect of bringing me closer to the truth, and of awakening me to a new awareness of the strength and beauty of my own Christian faith.

Being able to name and affirm the seeds of truth—those vital seeds of the Gospel—wherever they can be found in the present age, whether in the world of ideas or in contemporary culture in general, is a key part of the preacher's task. But a no less important task is being prepared, when necessary, to challenge popular culture, especially when it becomes the culture of death and the most vulnerable in our society come under direct assault. Wonderful, in this context, is what the American Catholic author Walker Percy has to say about the Church today and the task of evangelization. He writes, "By remaining faithful to its original commission, by serving its people with love, especially the poor, the lonely, and the dispossessed, and by not surrendering its doctrinal steadfastness, sometimes even the very contradiction of culture by which it serves as a sign, surely the Church serves culture best."[20]

Walker Percy was a convert to the Catholic faith, and it was that very steadfastness, he tells us, that drew him to the Church, the remarkable vision of Peter's rock holding fast "amid the tumultuous crosscurrents of culture and history."[21] But it is not only truth that has drawn people to the Church; it is also the reality of sheer goodness in so many of its members. The Church in every age, in every generation, grows mainly by attraction, and there is on earth almost

---

20. Walker Percy, "Culture, the Church, and Evangelization," in *Signposts in a Strange Land* (New York: Farrar, Straus and Giroux, 1991) 303.
21. Percy, 303.

nothing more attractive than the startling courage and beauty of real holiness. So the preacher has everything to learn from the saints. For the words of the saints are words on fire; they are words hallowed and sharpened by living witness, words of vision, words capable, in a dark hour, of summoning and awakening to new life and new hope those among our contemporaries, and among ourselves, who may at times be feeling despair or feeling lost.

The preacher of God's Word does not, of course, have to be a saint, but without at least some form of visible witness, without words hallowed by witness, without a language bolstered by deeds and dipped fresh and deep into the springs of faith-conviction, the words of the preacher will most likely never be able to touch the imagination of our contemporaries and will almost certainly, therefore, sound hollow and fall flat. Worth reading, in this context, are these inspired yet sobering words from Eric Hoffer's book *The True Believer*: "Those who would transform a nation or the world cannot do so by breeding and captaining discontent or by demonstrating the reasonableness and desirability of the intended changes or by coercing people into a new way of life. They must know how to kindle and fan an extravagant hope."[22]

Among our contemporaries, the truly great preachers are men and women whose lives have been radically changed by their encounter with the Word of God. Not only are their minds quickened to a new depth of awareness, but their very souls, one can say, are profoundly affected by the truth and beauty revealed to them. They are not unaware, of course, that to a great number of their contemporaries in the twenty-first century, they must appear as

22. Eric Hoffer, *The True Believer: Thoughts on the Nature of Mass Movements* (New York: Harper, 1951), 9.

fools: so extravagant is the claim they make, so bold their vision. And yet they dare to speak with conviction of the power and beauty of the cross and Resurrection. Having once encountered Christ in living faith, nothing can negate the beauty that has seized them. No dominant new philosophy, no seductive dictatorship of ideas, will ever be able to distract them from their purpose or undermine for a moment the joyous folly of their enthusiasm.

CHAPTER THREE

Dominican Wisdom and the Dark Night[1]

There are certain words that are generally recognized as hallowed or sacred in the Dominican tradition, words such as preaching, democracy, contemplation, wisdom, and freedom. And, of course, another small word with an irrefutable claim to be added to the list: happiness! But why introduce into a reflection on Dominican spirituality a phrase such as "the dark night"? At first hearing, it evokes a spirituality altogether at odds with the robust and joyous Dominican way. It seems, in fact, to indicate a path of life and of prayer far more introverted and intense—and far more *tense*—than the common path that has been pursued over the centuries by most Dominicans.

When we think about Dominican preaching or Dominican wisdom, what comes to mind is not an abyss of darkness—not the "dark night"—but rather a certain light of understanding, an urgent yet serene knowledge of the Word, a radiance of truth. With regard to prayer, therefore, it was no surprise to discover that Peraldus, a friar preacher of the thirteenth century, instead of speaking about

1. A talk given originally as an Aquinas Lecture, Dominican University (River Forest, IL, February 28, 2008).

the tough interior challenges of the contemplative life, simply and boldly declared, "Prayer is such an easy job!"[2]

Decades later, however, in the fourteenth century, a decidedly different note was struck by three Dominican preachers in Germany: Johannes Tauler, Henry Suso, and Meister Eckhart. Time and time again, in their writing and preaching, the journey to God is described more in terms of darkness than light. How are we to explain the use by these Dominicans of such intense, dramatic language and, along with that, the overwhelming emphasis placed by them on the challenges of the contemplative journey? The first thing to note is that in the Rhineland at this time, the received pattern and vision of Dominican spirituality, a tradition acknowledged generally to be both balanced and outgoing, came under the influence of an inward-looking spirituality that had its roots in the Neoplatonism of Pseudo-Dionysius.

As the Dionysian influence took hold, was the Dominican approach, the instinctive Dominican way, radically undermined, changed beyond recognition? I would say, yes, changed, and for a period very profoundly changed, but not changed beyond recognition. At its ordinary best, Dominican spirituality has an ability to reshape itself in response to new circumstances while holding fast to certain critical core values, to respond without unnecessary prejudice or fear to whatever happens to be the most urgent, most challenging reality in the world at any given time, to refuse to be intimidated by the thread or counter-thread of the new.

An example from the thirteenth century of a notable reshaping of the first Dominicans' vision of things comes to mind. For several

2. William Peraldus, "Sermon on Prayer," in *Early Dominicans: Selected Writings*, ed. Simon Tugwell (New York: Paulist, 1982), 167.

years, the Dominican Constitution had made clear that the friars were not to read the works of pagan authors, an ordinance that effectively banned the reading of Aristotle, among others. In time, however, inspired by the bold, exploratory writings of Albert the Great and Thomas Aquinas, this section of the Constitution was removed and never subsequently restored. This revolution of attitude toward the reading of secular authors would in time prove to be of incalculable benefit both for the Dominican Order and for the wider Church.

But can the same be said regarding the impact of Pseudo-Dionysian spirituality on the Rhineland preachers of the fourteenth century? How transformative for Dominican spirituality was the new and striking attention given by Eckhart, Tauler, and Suso to the daunting and dark challenges of the faith journey? In order to answer this question satisfactorily and to help maintain a balanced perspective on these three remarkable authors, it will be necessary in what follows to offer some general assessment of their individual lives and writings.

MEISTER ECKHART

During his lifetime, Eckhart was a tremendously important but also notably controversial figure. Today, for our own age, particularly in the field of spirituality, he remains a figure no less important, no less controversial. Many of the things that he says in his sermons and treatises linger in the mind long after one has first read them. He is, one could say, as much a poet as a preacher. He has no hesitation in making deliberately provocative claims, his ideas and words lit by startling images and vivid paradoxes. No wonder, then, that some of his own contemporaries had difficulty on occasion in following the drift of his teaching.

Not untypical of Eckhart's ecstatic preaching style is the following remarkable declaration: "When I enter the ground, the bottom, the river and fount of the Godhead, none will ask me whence I came or where I have been. No one missed me, for there God unbecomes."[3] At this point in his sermon, Eckhart suddenly stops, as if becoming aware of the furrowed brows of the listeners down beneath him, his high ecstasy of thought giving way at once to a tone of playful and exuberant self-awareness: "Whoever has understood this sermon, good luck to him. If no one had been here I should have had to preach it to this offertory box!"[4]

Eckhart's high, unconstrained rhetoric and unwillingness (or incapacity) at times to control the beautiful, wild exuberance of his thought and vision cost him dearly in the end. He was accused of heresy, and certain of his teachings (within one diocese) were condemned by the Church. He himself was never excommunicated, nor did the Church ever forbid the reading of his works. What's more, although the condemnation has never been officially abrogated, his own personal fidelity to orthodox belief is today almost universally acknowledged. According to Hans Urs von Balthasar, for example, Eckhart's experience of God is "wholly limpid and shadowless."[5] Yes, it needs to be divested of some of its "unsuitable garments" of expression, but nevertheless, Eckhart's vision remains, Balthasar declares, "authentically Christian even in its most daring

---

3. Meister Eckhart, "Sermon 56," in *The Complete Mystical Works of Meister Eckhart*, ed. and trans. Maurice O'C. Walshe (New York: Crossroad, 1992), 294.

4. "Sermon 56," 294.

5. Hans Urs von Balthasar, *The Glory of the Lord: A Theological Aesthetics*, vol. 5, *The Realm of Metaphysics in the Modern Age*, trans. Oliver Davies et al. (Edinburgh: T&T Clark, 1991), 30.

conceptions."[6] St. John Paul II, at a private audience in September 1985, drew attention to the phenomenon of German and Flemish mysticism: "I think of the marvelous history of Rheno-Flemish mysticism of the thirteenth and especially the fourteenth centuries." Then he commented briefly on the distinctive character of Meister Eckhart's mysticism:

> Did not Eckhart teach his disciples: "All that God asks you most pressingly is to go out of yourself . . . and let God be God in you." One could think that in separating himself from creatures, the mystic leaves his brothers, humanity, behind. The same Eckhart affirms that, on the contrary, the mystic is marvelously present to them on the only level where he can truly reach them, that is, in God.[7]

If, encouraged by this statement of John Paul, some men and women of devotion decide to read Eckhart and expect to find work distinguished throughout by a focus on the most telling, most concrete details of the spiritual journey, they might well be disappointed, coming instead upon multiple pages of the Meister's work so exalted and so daring in speculation that, at times, not even the finest scholars are sure of their meaning. Should, however, our interested readers persist in their endeavor, a different Eckhart will gradually be revealed, an author whose work will succeed in capturing and holding their attention, whose vision of the spiritual

6. Balthasar, 30. For a positive assessment of Eckhart's mysticism, see Alois M. Haas, *Eckardus Theutonicus, homo doctus et sanctus: Nachweise und Berichte zum Prozess gegen Meister Eckhart* (Fribourg, CH: Universitätsverlag Freiburg Schweiz, 1992).

7. John Paul II, "Discourse given at a private audience to participants attending a colloquium on Adrienne von Speyr," *L'Osservatore Romano*, October 28, 1985, 9.

path is so illumined on occasion, and so fresh and down-to-earth, that it can be regarded as a mysticism of the everyday.

Here, for example, is Eckhart writing on two of his most important themes: the immediacy of God's presence to humanity and the urgent character of divine compassion.

A person can turn away from God; but no matter how far a person goes from God, God stands there on the lookout for him and runs out to meet him unawares.[8]

As godly repentance lifts itself up to God, sins vanish into God's abyss, faster than it takes me to shut my eyes, and so they become utterly nothing, as if they had never happened, if repentance is complete.[9]

If a man humbles himself, God cannot withhold his own goodness but must come down and flow into the humble man, and to him who is least of all he gives himself the most of all, and he gives himself to him completely.[10]

Whoever really and truly has God, he has him everywhere, in the street, and in company with everyone, just as much as in church or in solitary places or in his cell.[11]

---

8. Meister Eckhart, "Sermon 14," in *Meister Eckhart: Teacher and Preacher,* ed. Bernard McGinn (New York: Paulist, 1986), 274.
9. Meister Eckhart, *Counsels on Discernment* 12, in *Meister Eckhart: The Essential Sermons,* trans. E. Colledge and B. McGinn (New York: Paulist, 1981), 263.
10. Meister Eckhart, "Sermon 22," in *Essential Sermons,* 195.
11. Meister Eckhart, *Counsels on Discernment* 6, in *Essential Sermons,* 251.

But a person who is not at home with inward things does not know what God is. It is just like a man who has wine in his cellar and, having neither drunk nor even tried it, does not know that it is good. This is exactly the situation of people who live in ignorance. They do not know what God is and they think and fancy they are really living.[12]

When Eckhart addresses the question of knowing God, one word that he uses quite often in his preaching and writing is the word "darkness." Unfortunately, the exact meaning he intends to communicate with this word is not always clear, and this can be a cause of considerable bewilderment for those listening. To his enormous credit, however, in one of his sermons, Eckhart allows us to hear the voice of an individual who is clearly frustrated at not being able to understand what the Meister is talking about: "But what is this darkness? What do you call it? What is its name?"[13] And again: "Is that the best thing for me to do—to raise my mind to an unknowing knowledge that can't really exist? . . . Am I supposed to be in total darkness?"[14] Eckhart answers at once and without the least hesitation: "Certainly. You cannot do better than to place yourself in darkness and in unknowing."[15]

For Eckhart, the spiritual life is, first and last, a journey into the unknown, a journey beyond the ordinary frontiers of human understanding, something that will require, therefore, leaving behind the familiar, lit world of our human understanding. "In the Book of Love," he writes, referring to a text in the Song of Solomon, "the

---

12. Meister Eckhart, "Sermon 10," in *Teacher and Preacher*, 262.
13. Meister Eckhart, "Sermon 4," in *Complete Mystical Works*, 56.
14. Eckhart, 56.
15. Eckhart, 56.

soul speaks a short verse: 'All through the night I searched in my bed for him whom my soul loves, and I did not find him' (Song of Sol. 3:1)."[16] Eckhart comments, "The soul's searching in its bed can be interpreted to mean that whoever clings to or depends on anything which is beneath God, that person's bed is too confining."[17] Meister Eckhart is encouraging us here, as so often in his work, to get up, once and for all, out of the comfortable bed of our old ways of thinking and acting. And this "getting up," we are told, will require nothing less than a radical detachment, first from the warm comfort blanket of familiar but wholly inadequate thoughts and feelings about God, and second from all the different things in our immediate world to which we have become enslaved. Eckhart, of course, knows well that as vulnerable, finite beings, we are afraid of this detachment, afraid to launch out into the darkness of the unknown. But it is precisely, he insists, in the bewildering dark that our eyes will at last begin to see. What to us feels like a veritable death, the loss of all that was once clear—a blindness of bewilderment—marks, in fact, the beginning of a new life of wisdom and holiness. "Where understanding and desire end there is darkness, and there God's radiance begins."[18]

Something of the bold challenge of Eckhart's thinking finds a notable echo in a poem by the contemporary American author Edward Hirsch. Here are lines from the last two stanzas of his poem "For the Sleepwalkers":

---

16. Meister Eckhart, "Sermon 71," in *Teacher and Preacher*, 321.
17. Eckhart, 321–322.
18. Meister Eckhart, "Sermon 80," in *Complete Mystical Works*, 398.

> We have to learn the desperate faith of sleep-
> walkers who rise out of their calm beds
> and walk through the skin of another life.
> We have to drink the stupefying cup of darkness
> and wake up to ourselves, nourished and surprised.[19]

The place in his work where Eckhart offers the fullest explanation of what he means by "darkness" is his *Commentary on Exodus* and, in particular, his reflection on verse 21 of chapter 20: "Moses went into the darkness wherein God was."[20] The word "darkness" Eckhart interprets here as referring primarily to the overwhelming impact on the contemplative—on Moses in this case—of the astounding light of God's presence. But that, as it happens, is not the first meaning Eckhart gives to the word darkness. "You can also say," he writes, "that 'Moses drew near' to God in the darkness, because in darkness, that is in tribulation, man is compelled to have recourse to God and to invoke his help."[21]

According to the Carmelite mystic St. John of the Cross, writing two centuries later, darkness or the dark night refers to mysticism in the strict sense of the word and therefore to a very advanced stage on the spiritual journey. But here, Eckhart is content simply to declare that in the everyday dark and desolation of people's lives, God, although unseen, is somehow intimately close to them. He writes, "God is present to those who suffer, according to the Psalm: 'I am with the one in tribulation.'"[22] When Eckhart comes, moments later, to interpret the passage about Moses and darkness in relation

19. Edward Hirsch, *For the Sleepwalkers* (New York: Alfred A. Knopf, 1987), 34.
20. Meister Eckhart, *Commentary on Exodus* 237, in *Teacher and Preacher,* 117.
21. Eckhart, 117.
22. Eckhart, 117.

to the contemplative or mystical life, he notes that "darkness" is to be understood "as the immensity and surpassing excellence of the divine light, according to the text of 1 Timothy 6: 'He dwells in light inaccessible.'"[23] "God," Eckhart declares, "is truly hidden from us in cloud and darkness." But this does not mean, he explains, "that obscurity covers God because with him there is no obscurity, but clear light according to the saying, 'The earth was illumined by his glory.'"[24] And so, when we read of Moses or of the contemplative entering "into the darkness," this means, Eckhart explains, entering "into the surpassing light that beats down and darkens our intellect."[25] And he notes further, "We see the same thing when our eyes are beaten down and darkened by the rays from the sun's disk. This is also what Dionysius says in the first chapter of the *Mystical Theology*."[26]

Here, the most immediate concern of Eckhart is not to offer his readers or listeners an extended *psychological* analysis of the experience of spiritual darkness. That, in time, will be the special gift and concern—indeed the unique genius—of the Carmelite mystics. What holds Eckhart's attention, first and last, as a thinker and as a preacher, is not so much the fascinating, psychological transformation of *human* nature under grace, but rather simply the awesome power and exuberance, the beauty and transcendence, of the divine nature. In one sermon, Eckhart makes bold to declare: "The brightness of the divine nature is beyond words."[27] And, in another place, referring to what he calls "the silent darkness of the

23. Eckhart, 117.
24. Eckhart, 117.
25. Eckhart, 117.
26. Eckhart, 117–118.
27. Meister Eckhart, "Sermon 53," in *Essential Sermons,* 203.

hidden Fatherhood," he writes, "God remains there within himself, unknown, and the light of the eternal Father has eternally shone in there, and the darkness does not comprehend the light."[28]

Reading or hearing these remarkable statements, one might conclude that Eckhart, as a theologian, is resigned never to declare anything positive about God—content, that is, simply to repeat over and over again the great *via negativa* assertions concerning the divine nature. But, strange to say, it is the very thought of the transcendence of God—thought straining *beyond* thought—that seems somehow to quicken and compel the imagination of the preacher. One has the impression at times that Eckhart is barely able to contain the surge, the welling up into his mind, of words and images. In one sermon, for example, he doesn't hesitate to compare the exuberant energy of God to that of a horse let loose into a field and jumping about in a sheer ecstasy of freedom. God, Eckhart tells us, finds enormous delight in pouring himself out in nature and in all created things: "It is just as enjoyable for him as when someone lets a horse run loose on a meadow that is completely level and smooth. Such is the horse's nature that it pours itself out with all its might in jumping about the meadow. This it would find delightful; such is its nature. So, too, does God find delight and satisfaction."[29]

Eckhart was highly regarded by his Dominican contemporaries and, in particular, by the two contemporary friars preachers most celebrated for holiness of life, Johannes Tauler and Bl. Henry Suso. Even after Eckhart was condemned, Tauler chose to refer to him as a "dear teacher," someone, he suggested, who had been greatly misunderstood: "One dear teacher taught you . . . and you did not

28. Meister Eckhart, "Sermon 22," in *Essential Sermons,* 196.
29. Meister Eckhart, "Sermon 12," in *Teacher and Preacher,* 269.

understand him. He spoke from the point of view of eternity and you understood him from the point of view of time."[30] The loyalty expressed here for a revered master and a fellow Dominican is, of course, admirable. But Tauler does not hesitate, on occasion, to distance himself from some of the more extreme formulations or actual imbalances in Eckhart's teaching. He does this not to reject but rather to try to protect the great work and wisdom of Eckhart from unnecessary opposition and negative attack. Tauler, it has to be said, was nothing if not prudent. Accordingly, he felt constrained in one particular homily to acknowledge that Eckhart was not always wise in the way he communicated his vision, advocating a route to holiness "without guidance on uncharted paths."[31] Nevertheless, in that same homily, Tauler has no hesitation in referring to Eckhart as a "noble master," a tribute well judged.[32] For the Meister's aim was unquestionably noble. Over and over again, it's true, Eckhart unsettled the minds of his contemporaries, but his aim in doing this, in constantly disrupting their fixed and settled vison of things, was to lead them, in thought and spirit, to a place of great freedom and to a higher, more wise, more lasting, more wondrously radiant knowledge.

JOHANNES TAULER

Tauler was born around 1300 in Strasbourg, one of the Rhineland's flourishing cities. While still a teenager, around the year 1315, he entered the Dominican Order. Unlike Meister Eckhart, many of whose ideas he absorbed with enthusiasm, Tauler, for all his natural

30. Quoted in *Essential Sermons*, 16.
31. Quoted in Oliver Davies, *Meister Eckhart: Mystical Theologian* (London: SPCK, 1991), 218.
32. Davies, 218.

brilliance, was not an academic. He was a preacher first and last. A number of the things that he says in his sermons suggest that he was somewhat wary of intellectuals and more than a little suspicious of book learning.

One of his manifest gifts as a preacher and teacher was his ability to keep faith with some of the most challenging and most beautiful and transcendent aspects of the Eckhartian vision and, at the same time, to offer to those of his contemporaries who came to hear him speak a guidance that was not only eminently wise but also eminently practical and down-to-earth. This meant, in practice, showing a rather more detailed interest in the experiential aspects of Christian prayer than we find in the work of Eckhart. In fact, it is possible to think of Tauler as a sort of bridge between the high philosophical mysticism of Eckhart and the more empirical or psychological mysticism of the great Carmelites.[33]

The eighty-four sermons of Tauler that have survived enjoyed a very considerable influence not only on German-speaking countries but also on almost all of Europe. And that's not surprising. One of the manifest strengths of Tauler's preaching is the way his words, though marked by a sober, meditative style, are clearly aflame with the love of God. Here is a passage delivered by Tauler toward the end of a sermon on the Holy Trinity:

> Should you forget everything that has been said here, keep in mind these two little points: First, be truly humble, throughout your whole being . . . and see yourself honestly for what you are. And secondly, let the love you bear God be a true one . . . a love

---

33. That the writings of Tauler may have had a significant influence on St. John of the Cross and, in particular, on John's concept of the "dark night" has been discussed by a number of scholars. See, for example, Jean Orcibal, *Saint Jean de la Croix et les mystiques rhéno-flamands* (Paris: Desclée, 1966).

that embraces God most ardently. Such love is a far cry from what is usually meant by religious feeling, which is situated in the senses. What I mean here transcends all sensible experience; it is a gazing upon God with one's entire spirit, a being drawn by love, just as a runner is drawn, or an archer, who has a single goal before his eyes.[34]

In another sermon, for the Fifth Sunday after Trinity, Tauler speaks of how God "flooded the whole of creation with His unfathomable mercy . . . and how the Most Blessed Trinity has awaited us to share in its eternal joy."[35]

When we reflect on all this with profound love, a great and active joy will be born in us. And whoever reflects on these matters lovingly will be overwhelmed by such interior joy that his feeble body cannot contain it, and it results in a special outburst of joy. . . . Thus it is granted to us to taste how sweet the Lord is, and we experience union with God in a special embrace. So God attracts, invites, and draws us out of ourselves, from a state of unlikeness into one of likeness.[36]

In order to bring home to his listeners the full practical reality of God's love for struggling sinners, Tauler does not shy away at times from using the most basic colloquial language and somewhat crude imagery. On one occasion, he compares the faults that an individual cannot rid himself of with the dung that a horse carries to fields,

34. Johannes Tauler, "Sermon 29," in *Johannes Tauler: Sermons*, trans. Maria Shrady (New York: Paulist, 1985), 108.
35. Johannes Tauler, "Sermon 40," in *Tauler: Sermons*, 142.
36. Tauler, 142.

where, in time, the dung itself will help produce "fine wheat and sweet good wine." This growth, he states, would never flourish in this way "if the dung were not there." And so, he concludes, "Now, your own faults, of which you cannot rid yourself or overcome are your dung. These you should carry with much effort and labor to the field of God's will in true detachment from yourself. Scatter your dung on this noble field and, without any doubt, there shall spring up noble and delightful fruit."[37]

Other parts of Tauler's work take up the theme of detachment and are radical in their insistence on the need for all those listening to make a journey within, turning their attention away from all the things that distract them from God. It was a demanding message, and yet it attracted large numbers of people. What was it that drew them? Already, in this chapter, the influence on the Rhineland contemplatives of Pseudo-Dionysius has been noted. But I think there is an even more important factor to be considered, and that's the clearly unstable and profoundly anxious character of society at that time. Most of Europe in those decades was reeling with major distress, subject to frequent famines, earthquakes, floods, and other natural calamities, not least among them the Black Death.

> It was a restless age, unsure of itself and unsure of political realities and religious values that had seemed unquestionable in the centuries immediately preceding. . . . It is hardly surprising, then, that when faced with conditions so full of uncertainty and so lacking in promise many "turned inward." The internal workings of the soul became the focal point of attention. . . .

37. Johannes Tauler, "Sermon 6," in *The Rhineland Mystics: An Anthology,* ed. and trans. Oliver Davies (London: SPCK, 1989), 86.

What differentiates fourteenth-century spirituality from that of other times is that this deep concern with the interior life gripped relatively large numbers of people, both clergy and laity, and that the pursuit of inwardness became such an intense and exclusive goal for so many.[38]

One striking manifestation of this pursuit was the flourishing in the German Rhineland of a great number of Dominican contemplative communities of nuns. The friars, chosen to work as chaplains or as spiritual guides to the nuns, were inevitably drawn to reflect, at a new depth, at a new theological level, on the drama of the interior life and on the steps and stages of the soul's journey to God. As a result, it is no exaggeration to say that the mystical teaching of the Rhineland Dominicans was, in large measure, the fruit of "a collaborative effort" between the nuns and the friars.[39]

One of the devices Tauler employed when he was preaching in order to cast light on the impact of God was to take a phrase or an image from the Gospels and use it as a metaphor for the interior journey. Thus, commenting on the image of "the lost coin" in Luke's Gospel, Tauler notes that, in a manner similar to the way the woman searches desperately for her "lost coin," God likewise searches the inner heart of the believer. He writes, "As soon as we enter our house to search for God there, God in His turn searches for us, and the house is turned upside down. He acts just the way we do when we

---

38. Frank Tobin, introduction to *Henry Suso: The Exemplar, with Two German Sermons* (New York: Paulist, 1989), 14–15.

39. One indication of this collaboration is the fact that a certain medieval text which, until recently, had been attributed solely to the work of Henry Suso is now known to have been penned, at least in part, by one of the nuns of the Convent of Töss, a friend of Suso, called Elsbeth Stagel. See Richard Woods, *Mysticism and Prophecy: The Dominican Tradition* (London: Darton, Longman & Todd, 1998), 110.

search for something: throwing aside one thing after another, until we find what we are looking for."[40]

The impact on our hearts and minds of this divine searching is purifying and profound. It subverts many, if not indeed *all*, of our old ways of thinking and feeling. Tauler writes, "If God seeks us and turns this house upside down, all the modes and manners which have enabled us in the past to form a rational concept of Him must be abandoned. . . . Everything must be reversed so radically as if we had never had any concept of God at all."[41] What Tauler is describing here is a phenomenon that later contemplatives and scholars would come to regard as a core aspect of the "dark night."

Apart from the image of "the coin," there are other Gospel images selected by Tauler to help describe the impact of God on the soul. Here are two of them: the image of "myrrh" in Matthew 2:11 (Sermon 3) and of "winter" in John 10:22 (Sermon 13).

The Myrrh of Suffering: First Sermon for Epiphany
"And opening their treasures, they offered Him gifts: gold, frankincense and myrrh (Matt. 2:11)." [42] At the time of Christ, myrrh was a perfume that, among other things, was used to anoint the dead. Here, in the infancy narrative of Matthew, it serves as a symbol of the suffering and death that Christ as an adult would undergo. Tauler,

40. Johannes Tauler, "Sermon 37," in *Tauler: Sermons,* 126. For a more extended reflection on this passage from Tauler, see Paul Murray, *In the Grip of Light: The Dark and Bright Journey of Christian Contemplation* (London: Bloomsbury, 2012), 95–97.

41. Tauler, 126.

42. Johannes Tauler, "Sermon 3, First Sermon for Epiphany." Unfortunately, a complete collection of the sermons of Tauler does not exist in English translation, and there are no trustworthy English translations of either Sermon 3 or Sermon 13. It has been helpful, therefore, to consult the French translation of the complete sermons of Tauler. See *Sermons: Jean Tauler: édition intégrale,* ed. Jean-Pierre Jossua, trans. É. Hugueny, G. Théry, and M.A.L. Corin (Paris: CERF, 1991), 27–32.

in his sermon for the Feast of the Epiphany, focuses his attention throughout on the reality of suffering in the Christian life. His message is extremely tough but greatly encouraging.

He speaks of "the myrrh of suffering" that God gives, a "myrrh" that is bitter to taste but, once accepted *with love,* quickens in the inmost depth of the soul great joy and peace. "Whether God sends you suffering little or great, it is from the depths of His unspeakable love; and in this He gives you something more useful than any gift; namely His very love itself."[43]

On occasion, men and women of devoted prayer and great goodness are tested, Tauler notes, in "astonishing and quite extraordinary ways," a testing that can take the form of "intense anguish and interior darkness."[44] As a result, and not surprisingly, they sometimes go to Tauler and exclaim, "Master, what dryness in my inner self, what appalling darkness!" But Tauler reassures them, declaring, "You will find you are much better off on account of this bitterness than if you had received great sweetness."[45] It's a teaching that's by no means easy to accept. Those most inclined to oppose it, Tauler notes, are people who regard themselves as more intelligent than others. "Some people think themselves so wise that they can ward off affliction by their own good management. . . . They want to be wiser than God, to teach God what to do and how to do it. . . . Such people suffer a great deal, but their myrrh only makes them more bitter. . . . That's why simple people often progress much faster in the spiritual life than people relying on the high notions of their reason."[46]

43. Tauler, 28.
44. Tauler, 30.
45. Tauler, 30–31.
46. Tauler, 31.

Here, it might seem that Tauler is sounding an anti-intellectual note, but he goes on at once to say, "If these clever ones would only follow God and abandon themselves to him, they would progress further and more joyfully than the others because, at every turn, their reasoning powers would be a marvelous help to them."[47]

The Winter of the Soul: Thursday Before Palm Sunday

"It was winter, and the festival of the Dedication was being held (John 10:22)." The "Thursday" corresponds with the Feast of Dedication of the Temple in Jerusalem. Tauler, in his sermon, focuses attention not on the external "Festival of Dedication," but rather on the festival that's taking place within the soul. For, in the temple of the soul, he explains, there is "a true feast of dedication": "As often as a man enters his interior soul—even a thousand times a day if that were possible," a *renewal* takes place accompanied by a "new purity of intention, new light, new grace, and new virtues."[48]

"And it was winter" (John 10:22). "When is it really winter?"[49] Tauler asks, and he responds by saying that, in the spiritual life, there are two winters of deprivation when it appears that God is absent. The first is when a person has become so much a slave to external delights and pleasures that all contact with the inner life of the spirit is lost: "It is when the heart has grown cold; when it has within it neither grace, nor God, nor any Godlike things." The heart is, in effect, held fast by "snow and frost," by those corrupt, false, deceitful things that freeze and imprison the soul.[50]

47. Tauler, 31.
48. Johannes Tauler, "Sermon 13, Thursday before Palm Sunday," in *Sermons: Jean Tauler*, 99.
49. Tauler, 99.
50. Tauler, 100.

The second "winter," though superficially similar in appearance, belongs to an entirely different reality. It refers to an advanced stage in the contemplative journey and is experienced normally by men and women of prayer who are "mindful of God" but who begin to feel utterly and completely abandoned by God. It is a veritable winter of the spirit: "As far as feelings go, the individual is dry, dark and cold, devoid of all heavenly consolation and sweetness."[51] Nevertheless, Tauler has no doubt whatever that what is happening at this point is an experience profoundly graced. This spiritual winter, he claims, was in fact experienced by Christ Jesus. He also found himself "abandoned by his Father." During his "unspeakably bitter passion," in his poor human nature, he received "not the least drop of comfort" from the Godhead. He was "the most forsaken, most helpless, most suffering of men."[52]

Tauler then goes on to spell out clearly the enormous blessing that this cold and tenebrous winter of the spirit can achieve for God's true friends. Should they be able to follow their Shepherd through this dark winter, "God will be present to them in a manner far more useful to them than a full summer of [spiritual] joys and favors."[53] No one, he writes, can conceive of the good that lies hidden in this dark trial: "It is far beyond all the pleasurable experiences one could ever imagine."[54]

BLESSED HENRY SUSO

Born toward the end of the thirteenth century, Suso came from the South German province of Swabia. He joined the Dominican Order

51. Tauler, 100.
52. Tauler, 100.
53. Tauler, 100.
54. Tauler, 100.

while still a teenager, and five years later, he underwent a profound religious awakening. From that point on, his spiritual life was marked by a pattern of severe mortifications and by a notable series of visions and ecstasies, his spirituality grounded in the culture of piety and penance typical of the late medieval period. It's thought probable that, when he was a Dominican student at Cologne, young Henry sat at the feet of Meister Eckhart. That said, however, it's hard to imagine two Dominican authors more decidedly different in style and vision.

In Suso's autobiography, *The Life of the Servant*, we are introduced to a number of the different kinds of suffering and temptation that Suso endured during his life. As a challenge to his prayer and to his faith, "thoughts of despair would rise up in him and say accusingly, 'What good does it do you to serve God? You are cursed; there is no hope for you. Give it up now. You are lost no matter what you do.'"[55] Suso was clearly reduced to a sorry state. "Wretched man that I am, where shall I turn? . . . Dear God, was ever anyone worse off than I am?"[56] Eventually, he shared his inner torment with his close friend, the contemplative nun Elsbeth Stagel. It was she, Stagel, who was responsible for noting down all the details of the story. In the end, the problem was happily resolved with the help of none other than Meister Eckhart: "When this horrible suffering had been going on for about ten years, during which time [Suso] considered himself simply as a damned person, he went to the saintly Meister Eckhart and lamented to him his suffering. [Eckhart] helped him get free of

55. Henry Suso, *The Life of the Servant*, in *The Exemplar*, 105.
56. Suso, 105.

it, and thus he was released from the hell in which he had existed for so long a time."[57]

When some of Eckhart's writings were condemned by the Church, the news must have come as a great shock to Suso. All indications suggest, however, that he continued to hold Eckhart in the highest regard. Oliver Davies comments, "A personal testimony of this kind of a saintly man such as Suso who personally knew Meister Eckhart is a matter to posterity of no little significance."[58] In the *Life*, we are told that, after Eckhart's death, the great mystic and theologian actually appeared to Suso and delivered an astonishing message. The account reads, "Meister Eckhart informed him that [Eckhart] lived in overflowing glory in which his soul had been made utterly god-like in God."[59] Moments later, after a further brief conversation, Eckhart advised Suso that he "should adopt an attitude of calm patience toward all wolfish men."[60] Needless to say, this unexpected apparition must have confirmed Suso in his long-held conviction that Eckhart was a devoted and true man of God.[61]

Suso was the author of a number of books, but we have time to focus on only one of them: *The Little Book of Eternal Wisdom*. It was probably written between the years 1328 to 1330 and is by far the most accessible of all Suso's work for the modern reader. What makes it an engaging read is, first of all, the dialogue form in which it is written and, second, the fact that we hear throughout the work the personal voice of Suso. What we are being offered, line by line,

57. Suso, 105.
58. Oliver Davies, *God Within: The Mystical Tradition of Northern Europe* (London: Darton, Longman & Todd, 1988), 108.
59. Suso, *Life of the Servant*, 75.
60. Suso, 75.
61. Whether or not the figure of Suso's vision was Meister Eckhart has been the subject of some debate. See *The Exemplar*, 22, 378n20.

is not simply the thoughts a man had, as would be the case in a scholastic text, but rather a man having thoughts, a man in active, emotional, and thoughtful dialogue with God.

Considered simply as a work of literature, *The Little Book of Eternal Wisdom* is a remarkable achievement. According to Frank Tobin, "[Suso] reveals an awareness of the complexities of literary form and its relation to meaning that one otherwise finds only in the most celebrated medieval authors."[62] But literary excellence is not Suso's principal aim. Where his genius is most evident is in the way he is able to transform his own individual story and mystical experience into a preaching for the sake of others, a preaching that both challenges and inspires. His intention when he incorporates specific details of his own biography into the work is not to draw attention to himself, but rather to make eloquent the Gospel message. On this point, the medieval scholar Bernard McGinn writes, "[Suso] presents himself, his pious practices, visions and mystical experiences as exemplary of profound theological truths. His literary artistry, with its great gifts for narrative presentation and its rhetorical richness, is always in the service of a theological agenda."[63]

Suso, when he is introducing *The Little Book of Eternal Wisdom*, notes that the "intimate conversations" he held with Eternal Wisdom did not take place as "physical conversations or with responses perceptible through the senses."[64] The responses he "hears," in other words, are not private revelations but knowledge that has come "from the mouth of Eternal Wisdom—responses it spoke itself in the gospels—or from the most sublime teachers."[65] Suso then goes on to

62. Frank Tobin, introduction to *The Exemplar*, 51.
63. Bernard McGinn, Preface to *The Exemplar*, 5-6.
64. Henry Suso, *Little Book of Eternal Wisdom*, in *The Exemplar*, 208.
65. Suso, 208.

speak about the dialogue form of the work. The reason he chose this particular form, he says, is to make the subject "more interesting" for the reader. His aim is not to write as if he uniquely is "the one it pertains to or because he himself spoke it all about himself."[66] No, on the contrary, what he intends to present is "common teaching in which both he and everyone else can find what applies to them."[67]

Chapter 10 of *The Little Book* bears the striking title "Why God allows his friends to have such a bad time of it on earth." Referring to himself as "the servant," Suso starts by questioning God directly regarding this "bad time":

> I have a concern in my heart. May I speak to you about it? O dear Lord, if only I might dare, with your leave, to argue with you as the holy Jeremiah did. Gentle Lord, do not be angry, and listen patiently. Lord, people say: No matter how intensely sweet your love and intimacy are, still you often allow things to go quite badly for your friends. . . . After a person has entered into friendship with you, the next is that he prepare himself and firmly resolve to accept suffering. Lord, by your goodness, what sweetness can they enjoy in that? Or how can you allow all this in the case of your friends? Or is it something I am not allowed to know?[68]

Eternal Wisdom replies, "As my Father loves me, so do I love my friends. I treat my friends now as I have from the beginning of the world until this very day." This reply does not satisfy Suso for a moment. He answers, "Lord, that is exactly what people complain

66. Suso, 208.
67. Suso, 208.
68. Suso, 237.

about. This is why they say you have so few friends: because you let things go so badly for them in this world."[69] What Suso has in mind at this point are the many kinds of "bitter suffering" so often endured by the friends of God. In particular, he speaks of "the contempt of the whole world and much opposition."[70]

In an earlier chapter, Suso addresses another form of suffering endured by the friends of God, the cause, it would appear, of even greater anguish. It is that inner pain of spirit when it seems God has abandoned the soul and completely withdrawn the light of his presence. Here, once again, with a disarming directness, Suso bitterly complains to God about this withdrawal. He writes, "O Lord, if I dare say so, you ought to be a bit more true to these poor loving hearts that languish and consume themselves with desire for you, that send up so many deep sighs to you, their only Love, that look up toward you in their misery and say in a trembling voice: 'Come back! Come back!'"[71]

Sometimes it seems to Suso that God has all of a sudden returned to him: "My heart laughs," he says, "my spirits become light, my soul is full of joy."[72] But, then, just as quickly, God disappears once again: "Quickly, in an instant," Suso writes, "it is all snatched away and I am again naked and forsaken."[73] At this point, it all seems to be becoming too much for our Dominican brother. With barely disguised exasperation, Suso exclaims, "O Lord, are you the cause of this? Or am I? Or what is going on?"[74] God answers the question at

69. Suso, 237.
70. Suso, 237.
71. Suso, 234.
72. Suso, 235.
73. Suso, 236.
74. Suso, 236.

once and without hesitation. He says, "I am causing it. . . . It is the game of love."[75] Suso asks, "What is the game of love?" God replies, "As long as love is together with love, love does not know how dear love is. But when love departs from love, then truly love feels how dear love was."[76] The answer is certainly eloquent and very nicely phrased. But it doesn't win over Brother Henry. "Lord," he replies at once, "this is a tiresome game!"[77]

In making these comments, Suso may be relying in part on received knowledge from "sublime teachers" who wrote or spoke in similar vein concerning their own bewildering experience of the divine absence. But the stark honest words of complaint that we have just heard from Suso leave us with no doubt that what is being described is his own intimate, personal knowledge and experience of what would later be known popularly as the "dark night."

* * *

That Eckhart, Tauler, and Suso made an enormous contribution to the history of Western spirituality is universally acknowledged. Prior to the Carmelites of the sixteenth century, few authors in the Christian tradition explored in such depth the radiant dark mystery of God's absence or seeming absence in the life of prayer. All three are figures from a remote past, preachers of the fourteenth century. So, is it accurate to suggest that, for ourselves today in the twenty-first century, aspects of their work remain not only relevant but

---

75. Suso, 236. In the *Dialogue* of St. Catherine of Siena, another fourteenth-century text, the seeming absence of God experienced by people at prayer is referred to as "this lover's game of going and coming back." God the Father says to Catherine: "I call it a 'lover's game' because I go away for love and I come back for love—no, not really I, for I am your unchanging and unchangeable God; what goes and comes back is the feeling my charity creates in the soul" (*The Dialogue* 78, trans. Suzanne Noffke [New York: Paulist, 1980], 147).

76. Suso, *Little Book of Eternal Wisdom*, 236.

77. Suso, 236.

exemplary? The answer, in my judgement, is a strong and unqualified yes, and for the following reasons.

First, these three medieval Dominicans demonstrate the importance of individual and personal witness in the life of the preacher. When the words of a given preacher, a servant of the Word, are salted with the salt of lived experience, they immediately gain great authority. And the words of Eckhart, Tauler, and Suso are clearly instinct with that freshness and boldness that only direct and immediate experience can give.

Second, all three of the Rhineland preachers alert us to a hidden wisdom at the core of faith, a radiant yet dark knowledge of God. Like few others in the tradition, they are able to find words to describe the impact of God on the soul, knowledge that can help transform both prayer and preaching. At times, their ideas are so vivid and their words so bold and unexpected that whole lines or phrases can startle like lightning and go through us like a spear.

Third, the writings of Eckhart, Tauler, and Suso are greatly revered for their mystical depth, but these three medieval friars are a lot more than connoisseurs of the higher states and stages of the spiritual life. They are all three of them remarkable preachers of the Word.

Fourth, due, in part, to their contact with a great number of enclosed contemplative women, the Rhineland preachers can be said to possess that "experiential knowledge" described by Bl. Humbert of Romans in his treatise on preaching. "People," Humbert writes, "who have had much experience in dealing with the state of the human soul can say much about the affairs of the soul."[78]

78. Humbert of Romans, "Treatise on the Formation of Preachers" 2.9.4, in *Early Dominicans*, 217–218.

Fifth, because of the depth of their own faith experience, these three Rhineland Dominicans were able to offer enormous encouragement to those among their contemporaries who began to lose all sense of God, even finding themselves, on occasion, in what felt like a veritable darkness of unbelief. Regarding this matter, I have no doubt that many of our own contemporaries are in at least as much need of enlightenment and encouragement. Accordingly, we have much still to learn from the radiant dark wisdom of these three Dominican preachers of the fourteenth century, Eckhart, Tauler, and Suso.

CODA: A LOOK BACK TO THE FIRST FRIARS

The task of preaching in the early years of the Dominican Order's existence left little time for any kind of intense or extended reflection on the interior life. Simon Tugwell notes that "the early Dominicans were not particularly concerned, either for themselves or for others, with what has come to be called 'the interior life.' Some of them, certainly, were great men of prayer, but their prayer was simple, devotional and largely petitionary."[79] The overriding concern of Dominic and the early friars was to "be useful to the souls of others."[80] As a result, there was from the beginning an unmistakable "apostolic quality" about their prayers and devotions. In their dedicated lives of prayer, their aim was in every way possible to become better preachers.[81]

Clear evidence of this "apostolic quality" can be found in one of the earliest Dominican texts, *The Nine Ways of Prayer of Saint Dominic*, a work that affords us remarkably privileged access to the prayer life of the saint. Tugwell writes, "There seems no reason

79. Simon Tugwell, introduction to *Early Dominicans*, 3.
80. Prologue to "The Early Dominican Constitutions," in *Early Dominicans*, 457.
81. Tugwell, introduction to *Early Dominicans*, 4.

to doubt that, in the *Nine Ways,* we are in contact with the actual practice of prayer of St. Dominic, and with teaching that he gave to the brethren."[82] Dominic actively encouraged his brethren to pray for sinners. "There are many sinners," he would say, "to be directed towards mercy and love, for whose sake the prophets and apostles groaned in distress, and for their sake too Jesus wept bitterly when he saw them."[83]

One thing that can sometimes be overlooked in the reading of the *Nine Ways* is that, alongside the "apostolic quality" of Dominic's prayer, there was also indicated what can only be described as a mystical quality. Thus, in the brief paragraph of introduction to the *Nine Ways,* we are told that "apart from the common ways of prayer in the celebration of the Mass and in the prayer of psalmody in the canonical Hours, which he practiced very devoutly both in choir and when he was traveling," Dominic "often seemed suddenly to be caught up above himself to speak with God and the angels."[84] And again, in the Fourth Way of Prayer, we read, "Sometimes it seemed from the very way he looked that he had penetrated heaven in his mind, and then he would suddenly appear radiant with joy, wiping away the tears from his eyes."[85]

Earlier in that same Fourth Way of Prayer, we find Dominic citing lines from one of the Psalms, lines containing, it would seem, a hurt and troubled awareness of the absence or threatened absence of God: "To you, Lord, I will cry, do not turn away from me in silence,

---

82. *The Nine Ways of Prayer of Saint Dominic,* ed. and trans. Simon Tugwell (Dublin: Dominican, 1978), 6. There are two translations of the *Nine Ways of Prayer* by Tugwell. The first is this 1978 volume. The second is included in *Early Dominicans.*

83. "The Second Way of Prayer," in *Early Dominicans,* 96.

84. Tugwell, introduction to *The Nine Ways of Prayer,* in *Early Dominicans,* 94.

85. "The Fourth Way of Prayer," in *Early Dominicans,* 97

lest in your silence I become like those who go down into the pit" (see Ps. 28:1).[86] In the Sixth Way of Prayer, Dominic cites another passage no less vivid from the Psalms, a prayer at once suggestive of that paradoxical dryness of spirit so often experienced by the great contemplatives: "I have stretched out my hands to you. My soul is like soil without water before you, speedily hear me, Lord" (see Ps. 143:6–7).[87] It's worth noting that on these occasions, when citing Psalms 28 and 143, Dominic's focus of attention is not primarily on the state of his own soul, but rather on the need that certain others had at that time for the power of God's healing love and mercy—an urgent need for salvation in one case and the need for a miraculous healing in the other.[88]

The rare access we are given in *Nine Ways* to the inner prayer life of St. Dominic prompts a very interesting question. Did that life (and the spiritual life also of Dominic's fellow preachers), although mostly of a plain and devotional character, bear no resemblance whatever to the interior life described a century later by a Dominican preacher such as Johannes Tauler? Are there, in other words, any indications to suggest that, among these early friars, there were some who possessed a close and intimate knowledge about God's way of withdrawing his presence from the one seeking divine contact? Do we have evidence from those first years of that kind of mystical knowledge and insight?

Of all the early friars, no one, I would say, more accurately and impressively characterized early Dominican spirituality than Bl. Jordan of Saxony, the second Master of the Order. He was a

---

86. "The Fourth Way of Prayer," 97.
87. "The Fourth Way of Prayer," 99.
88. "The Fourth Way of Prayer," 97, and "The Sixth Way of Prayer," in *Early Dominicans*, 99.

preacher first and last, someone truly robust, good-humored, and outgoing. And yet it is Jordan, this joyful man, who demonstrates in his letters a telling awareness of certain aspects of what would later come to be known as the "dark night." It is Jordan who speaks of the mysterious withdrawal of God from the soul and of how the person at prayer seems to lose all feeling of love for God and all interest in the things of God. "The soul," Jordan says, writing to the community of his great friend, the Dominican nun Diana d'Andalò, "seeing and feeling her own hardness of heart, cries out: 'The Lord has forsaken me, the Lord has forgotten me.'"[89] But you have not been forgotten, Jordan insists: "If sometimes [Christ Jesus] seems to turn his face away from you and become a stranger to you, you must see this not as a punishment but as a grace."[90] In another letter, addressed to Diana and her community, he writes,

If any one of you be for a time cast down with weariness of spirit or afflicted with aridity of heart so that the torrent of devoted love seems to be dried up, will she dare to cry, My Lord has forsaken me and has no care for me, since the feelings of joy and devotion I have hitherto known are now gone from me? Such things must never be uttered by a bride of the gentle Christ Jesus: let them speak thus who know not his ways, nor how as I so often told you when I was with you, he is wont to kindle the love of his brides, how for a time he will draw away from you that you may seek him with greater ardor, and having sought may find him with

89. Jordan of Saxony, "Letter 20," in *To Heaven with Diana! A Study of Jordan of Saxony and Diana d'Andalò with a Translation of the Letters of Jordan*, trans. Gerald Vann (New York: iUniverse, 2006), 80.

90. Jordan of Saxony, "Letter 29," in *To Heaven with Diana*, 93.

greater joy, and having found may hold him with greater love, and having held may never let him go.[91]

A busy life of preaching afforded little or no time for penning reflections of this kind on the interior life. We can be grateful, therefore, that these few illumined thoughts of Jordan have survived. But if indeed the prayer of a devout believer can be as challenging on occasion as Jordan describes, does this not rather negate the notion that "prayer is such an easy job"?[92] When, in the thirteenth century, Peraldus made this declaration, he was not for a moment, I am sure, forgetting or ignoring the fact that the prayer life of the average Christian normally involves, at some point, a struggle with distractions and temptations. And Peraldus, for all we know, may also have been aware of other more testing trials in the life of prayer. But the simple genius and authority of the declaration "Prayer is such an easy job" remains valid all the same.

It serves to underline the fact that, at its core, authentic Christian prayer is not something reserved for a spiritual or pious elite. In a moment of desperation and need, for example, even the worst of sinners can attain, and with speed, to the very heart of prayer. Witness the cry of the Good Thief on the cross: "Jesus, remember me when you come into your kingdom!" (Luke 23:42). The fact that prayer is easy in the way suggested by this example is a belief, a Gospel conviction, with which Dominican preachers and theologians have boldly and unswervingly kept faith over the centuries.

But Dominicans such as Jordan of Saxony and the Rhineland contemplatives have clearly not been unaware of other aspects of

---

91. Jordan of Saxony, "Letter 20," 80.
92. William Peraldus, "Sermon on Prayer," in *Early Dominicans*, 167.

the interior life. Such contemplative insight, however, such living knowledge of the darkness of faith, though at times challenging and even bewildering, never for a moment robbed these men of the joy they had in praising God or of their wholehearted commitment to the task of preaching. On the contrary, it is precisely because with tenacity and unwavering hope they lived through the dark hours of prayer that their lives as preachers were so radiant and their writings of such great use and inspiration for others.

An overwhelming emphasis on the trials of the faith journey, an insistent focus on the dark night, is not of course what distinguishes the graced familiar path of Dominican spirituality. Nevertheless, our brief study has demonstrated that there does exist in the Dominican tradition a stream of wisdom and experience that names for us—helpfully and encouragingly—some of the most challenging, most humbling, and most difficult moments in the life of prayer. Moments such as these, moments of darkness, trial, and bewilderment, can, in the view of Bl. Jordan and the three Rhineland preachers, mark the start of a truly graced adventure into God: *Where understanding and desire end there is darkness, and there God's radiance begins.*

CHAPTER FOUR

Dominicans and the Key of Knowledge[1]

A Talk to Friars Studying in Rome

On this day of prayer and reflection, I have been asked to speak on a topic that's already familiar to you as Dominican friars. So, what can I hope to say this morning that's new, that's fresh, that's helpful? All I can do—and I'm honored and humbled to attempt it—is to share with you a few thoughts, a few loaves and fishes of insight. You yourselves, of course, will be able to bring to what I say your own thoughts, your own vision, and that encourages me to make a start.

TAKING HOLD OF THE KEY

What is the main motive, the principal reason, for being sent to Rome as Dominican friars to study at one or other of the pontifical universities? The answer is simple: it is, of course, to gain new knowledge. But how does this knowledge differ from the knowledge that students in secular universities are actively seeking, whether here in Rome or elsewhere in the world? There is a particular phrase that Christ uses in chapter 11 of St. Luke's Gospel, a tiny phrase but one that can, I think, assist us in answering the question. The phrase

1. Given originally on a day of retreat and reflection at the Angelicum (February 19, 2023).

occurs during a heated conversation that Christ had been having with certain scholars of his own generation, a group of lawyers. At one point, with a surprisingly strong, indeed almost fierce passion, Christ refers to something that he calls "the key of knowledge." What he has in mind is not, obviously, a form of academic knowledge that's merely static, but rather knowledge that transforms, knowledge that has the power to open a door into a new world of truth and freedom, knowledge that saves.

At one point, when Christ is speaking with the scribes, he is scarcely able to contain his anger. "Woe to you lawyers!" he exclaims. "For you have taken away the key of knowledge" (Luke 11:52). The reason Christ is so angry is because the group he is addressing, the scholars, although they had been offered the tremendous opportunity of receiving "the key of knowledge," didn't make the necessary effort to take hold of it. They were, it would seem, lazy and complacent. What's more, they managed to block the path of others of their generation, non-scholars presumably, who clearly wanted to enter into the house of knowledge but, in the end, were denied the chance. "You did not enter yourselves," Christ remarks to the scholars, "and you hindered those who were entering" (Luke 11:52).

Something of the urgency of Christ's statement I find echoed centuries later by Bl. Jordan of Saxony in an encyclical letter he sent out to the entire Order. Jordan was alarmed to discover that the younger men in formation were not committing themselves enough to their academic tasks. He was worried that, as a result, they might fail to grasp the Gospel vision and focus instead on their own private pieties and devotions. Should they do that, Jordan warns, the results will be grave. Apart from "neglecting their own benefit," they will, he notes, "deprive many people of a chance of salvation, when they could have helped them on their way to eternal life if only they had studied properly."[2]

A knowledge informed by the Gospel—redemptive knowledge—was of immediate and major concern to St. Dominic at the beginning of the Order. And that explains why he sent his young friars to the different universities of Europe, acting with an urgency and speed that was quite remarkable. Obviously, the circumstances of the hour had impressed upon Dominic that a great deal was at stake. He realized that the people of his own generation, like people in every generation, perish without a vision, without the help, in other words, of what Christ names "the key of knowledge."

With regard to yourselves, when the period of study in Rome has come to an end and you will have successfully, let's presume, passed all your exams, you will be awarded a well-deserved degree or diploma. And that, of course, will be no small joy, no small achievement. But there is something else you will be taking back home with you that is far more important than a diploma. A diploma, after all, or a degree, is something for yourself. But if, by happy providence of grace and hard work, your years in Rome enable you in the end to seize hold of "the key of knowledge," you will be able to return back to your different countries and provinces with a gift that is *for others*, a living knowledge of God and of the Gospel that will help open doors into a new freedom of spirit, a new depth of understanding, a new fullness of life.

2. Jordan of Saxony, "Encyclical Letter, May 1233," in *Early Dominicans: Selected Writings*, ed. Simon Tugwell (New York: Paulist, 1982), 123–124.

DOVES AND RAVENS: TWO KINDS OF STUDENT

Aquinas, in one of his biblical commentaries, contrasts two very different kinds of student: one he calls a raven and the other a dove. The "raven" is the student whose only real interest is his own intellectual fulfillment and satisfaction. In contrast, the other student is unselfish, a "dove" of charity and compassion, a man of prayer, someone who not only contemplates but who desires, and with great urgency, to share with others the fruits of his study and contemplation. The dove image St. Thomas found, of course, in the book of Genesis—the dove that returns speedily to the ark of Noah in order to bring the good news. In contrast, the raven, the self-absorbed academic, has no particular concern for the needs of others, no strong, active interest of any kind in what his neighbors may be enduring. Thomas writes,

> The raven did not turn back to the ark. But the dove returned bearing a green olive branch. Those fly like ravens who do not turn back to the ark by the affection of holiness, for they do not think of anything but themselves, namely, how they might track down some truth. . . . But those fly like doves who both contemplate and turn back towards their neighbors, teaching what they have contemplated, those who, with the green olive branch in their mouth, bear as porters the oil of mercy, devoting themselves to their neighbors.[3]

Fr. Vincent McNabb, a Dominican from Ireland but a member of the English Dominican Province all his life, remarked once while

---

3. Thomas Aquinas, "Psalm 54:5," in *S. Thomae Aquinatis Opera omnia*, vol. 6, *Reportationes*, ed. Roberto Busa (Stuttgart: Frommann-Holzboog, 1980), 128.

giving a talk to his Dominican brethren, "The world is waiting for those who love it. . . . If you don't love men and women don't preach to them—preach to yourself!"[4] None of us, as friars preachers, are sent to Rome to focus primarily on our own careers or to impress the people back home or to explore for our own pleasure some highly specialized area of academic research. Should I discover in time, however, that this is in fact the *main* motive driving me in my studies, then I will have become, or I will soon risk becoming, one of those selfish ravens of whom St. Thomas speaks. What's more, if, during the period of my studies, I don't possess at least something of the urgency felt by Dominic for the preaching task, if I am not contemplative day to day of the grave and pressing needs of my contemporaries and of the significance of my daily commitment to study in relation to those needs, then, almost certainly, I will have become as indifferent to the needs of others as the scribes and scholars at the time of Jesus.

A SPIRITUAL FAMINE

Given the truly desperate plight of so many of our contemporaries in the world, the studies we are undertaking here at the Angelicum and elsewhere in Rome might well appear, on occasion, to be somewhat detached from reality, a form almost of self-indulgence. Absorbed in our different academic tasks, it might seem to an outsider that we have no special interest in or concern for those among our contemporaries who are most in need of help. Should we, therefore, consider abandoning all our intellectual pursuits and devoting ourselves instead to answering as best we can the most pressing,

---

4. Spoken by McNabb during a retreat in 1927. See *An Old Apostle Speaks: Father Vincent McNabb,* ed. Gerald Vann (Oxford: Blackfriars, 1946), 3.

most immediate needs of the poorest of the poor in our society? That phrase, "poorest of the poor," brings at once to mind the life and work of St. Teresa of Kolkata. Many years ago, I remember, when I was studying here in Rome pursuing a licentiate degree in spirituality, Mother Teresa was invited to come and talk for half an hour to one of our classes. She spoke first about her work and about the hunger and degradation of the poor people whom she and her sisters were serving in Kolkata and elsewhere. But then she said something like this to the class, and I'll never forget it:

> Don't be looking back over your shoulder at the poverty of Kolkata, and at the work which we are trying to do there. Instead, realize that your God-given task for these years is to give your whole-hearted attention to the task of study. That is your vocation here and now, that is your call. Yes, the poor of the world are indeed starving for food, but there is another kind of starvation in the world, and it's no less profound, no less terrible. People are desperate to know the meaning of their lives, they are starving for the saving knowledge of God, they are starving for the truth that gives meaning, for the truth that saves and sets free. Who will answer that need, who will answer that hunger, if people like yourselves don't give their whole attention, during these privileged years, to an ever-deeper understanding of the Gospel vision? Don't be distracted from your task by looking back over your shoulder at the poverty of Kolkata. Attend here and now to that other grave hunger of spirit which exists everywhere in the world. Attend to the necessary, much-needed task which God has given you.

Yes indeed, famine can take many different forms. Bl. Humbert of Romans, in his "Treatise on the Formation of Preachers," draws our attention to a depth of hunger in society that should never be overlooked. "Man does not live by bread alone," he declares, repeating Christ's words, "but by every word which comes from the mouth of God." Without hesitation, therefore, Humbert asserts, "If preaching fails, there is spiritual famine."[5]

If today, as friars preachers, we are keen to address that famine, anxious to bring to those among our contemporaries who are spiritually starving the alms of truth and the bread of meaning, we need first and last to feed our own minds on that bread, on that truth. We need, in other words, as soon as we are made aware of our own poverty, to study in depth the Word of God, not as an isolated text but as a living truth, a wisdom that speaks like nothing else on earth to the needs of the present hour. For nowhere in the world can there be found a teaching that gives more complete and accurate attention to the most urgent needs of our contemporaries.

THE GRACE OF ATTENTION

"Attention." That word recurs a number of times in a remarkable document on study sent by Simone Weil in 1942 to her friend and spiritual confidant, the French Dominican Fr. Joseph-Marie Perrin. The document is titled "Reflections on the Right Use of School Studies with a View to the Love of God." At one point, speaking of the usefulness of studies, Weil makes bold to say, "The development of the faculty of attention forms the real object and almost the sole interest of studies."[6] And she adds, "Whoever goes through years

5. Humbert of Romans, "Treatise on the Formation of Preachers" 1.3.17, in *Early Dominicans*, 189.

6. Simone Weil, *Waiting on God*, trans. E. Craufurd (Glasgow: Collins, 1983), 66.

of study without developing this attention within himself has lost a great treasure."[7]

In similar vein, St. Albert the Great, in one of his homilies, speaks of the necessity of giving a very particular kind of attention to the needs of others. Commenting on St. Paul's invocation in Romans 12:15, "Rejoice with those who rejoice, weep with those who weep," Albert writes: "[St. Paul] means that . . . you should make your heart like your neighbor's heart, so that when he is happy, you are happy, and you grieve with him when he is grieving."[8]

What we might call the gift or grace of attention is described for us in the Acts of the General Chapter of Providence (2001) with one brief, telling phrase: "intellectual compassion." What the phrase suggests is that the essential point of Dominican study is to be able to share with others not simply truth in its unmoved, detached objectivity but truth in its most dynamic form—truth, in other words, in the form of a deeply intelligent and profoundly creative attention. *Misericordia Veritatis* is the phrase used in the text to describe it—"the Mercy of Truth." "Study," we are told, "helps us to perceive human crises, needs, longings, and sufferings as our own." And further, "The intellectual mission of the Order calls us to share not just the 'gaudium et spes' [the joy and hope], but also the 'luctus et angor' [the grief and anguish] of our time."[9]

That idea is not, of course, a new idea. It expresses, in fact, the manifestly wise understanding of the subject possessed many years ago here at the Angelicum by Bl. Hyacinth Cormier—the vision

---

7. Weil, 75.

8. Albert the Great, quoted in Simon Tugwell, "The Life and Works of Albert," in *Albert and Thomas: Selected Writings,* ed. Simon Tugwell (New York: Paulist, 1988), 36.

9. Prologue to "The Intellectual Life," in "Acts of the Elective Chapter of the Friars of the Order of Preachers, Providence," no. 109 (Rome, 2001), 46.

Cormier had of Dominican study when he helped refound our university. Cormier wrote, and his words leap off the page when we read them, "The study of the holy books [of Scripture] demand of us that we acquire the entrails of mercy and extend them."[10]

SCHOLARSHIP, FREEDOM, AND SANCTITY

All too often in contemporary spirituality, we are encouraged to believe that it is the heart that brings us close to those in affliction, not the mind, not the intelligence. As a result, time dedicated to study can be perceived as a positive hindrance to helping the needy and to the pursuit of holiness. Sometimes we are even encouraged to make a journey, an exodus, out from the captivity of the so-called dry and gray intellect to the fresh and living springs of the heart.

This dualism, however, between head and heart is something quite foreign to the Dominican spirit and understanding. Actual goodness, it is true, can certainly be considered as the holiness of the heart, since from there charity springs. But thinking, serious thinking about the Gospel and about the world we are living in, can itself be a form of holiness, and a necessary form. Accordingly, Dominicans in every age tend to insist that there can be no serious awakening to God without an awakening in the mind. For, as disciples of the Word, we discover at the end if not at the beginning of our studies that, whereas goodness may indeed be the holiness of the heart, truth is the holiness of the mind.

No small part of the intellectual discipline demanded of Dominicans who are called to higher studies is what we call scholarship. But what role exactly does scholarship play in the life of the Order

10. Hyacinth Cormier, *Le Père Cormier: Être à Dieu*, ed. Gilles Berceville and Guy Bedouelle (Paris: CERF, 1994), 128.

and in the life of the Church? How critical is its contribution? Simon Tugwell, in a short but insightful paper titled "Scholarship, Sanctity and Spirituality," points out that "scholarship helps to keep open or to re-open the options that are actually there in the church."[11] He recalls the fact that Teresa of Avila always preferred learned directors to merely pious ones. "Spiritual but unlearned directors were cramped by their own experience; they knew only one way to be Christian." In contrast, "Learned directors . . . were more free precisely because of their learning, more *free* to recognize as legitimate ways of being Christian which were not part of the prevailing ethos."[12] The reality is, of course, that people will often be swayed by the fashions of their own age. And this holds true for spirituality as for everything else. What scholarship, at its ordinary best, can help us to see is that the authentic Gospel tradition is not limited by the dominant fashions of thought and feeling of one particular generation.

THE ADVENTURE OF STUDY

The most notable example in Dominican history of a scholar and theologian whose work helped liberate his own and later generations from the tyranny of a single vision is St. Thomas Aquinas. His first biographer, William of Tocco, stresses the newness of Thomas' approach to almost everything. "In his lectures," Tocco writes, "he raised *new* questions, and discovered a *new* and clear way of solving them, and he used *new* arguments in arriving at these solutions."[13] A major part of our inheritance as Dominicans is the Thomist tradition,

---

11. Simon Tugwell, "Scholarship, Sanctity and Spirituality," an address given at Gonzaga University in the United States and published in pamphlet form (Spokane, WA: 1983), 3.

12. Tugwell, "Scholarship, Sanctity and Spirituality," 4.

13. William of Tocco, *Vita s. Thomae Aquinatis*, in *Fontes vitae s. Thomas Aquinatis*, Fasc. 2, ed. D. Prümmer (Toulouse, 1924), 81. Emphasis added.

a gift that's of almost incalculable worth. But, needless to say, neither Thomism nor its most celebrated text, the *Summa theologiae*, should ever be presented as a fixed book of answers. That would suggest to students of philosophy and theology engaged in the search for truth that there is no longer any adventure left, as if truth itself, centuries ago, had already been fully known, systematized, and expressed in eternally fixed formulae.

This was not what Thomas Aquinas believed—not for a moment—nor was it the vision of Dominicans after him such as Catherine of Siena, Johannes Tauler, Bartolomé de Las Casas, Réginald Garrigou-Lagrange, and Yves Congar. In this context, I find it rather sad but also somewhat hilarious to recall a comment made on the *Summa* several decades ago by a certain Dominican archbishop. Talking to a group of novices, he declared, "Make sure that all of you read the *Summa* of Aquinas. It contains fifty-six thousand answers to all those who criticize the Catholic Church!"

St. Thomas, if he heard that declaration, would surely turn in his grave!

What, then, should be the aim of Dominican friars studying in Rome? First and last it should, of course, be to grow in knowledge of the living dogmatic and spiritual tradition of the Church, something that requires not only hard work and a healthy spirit of passionate inquiry but also a fundamental spirit of humility. If, however, real growth is to take place, what must also be in play in this process of learning are the questions that have been provoked by the student's own experience. In the eighth of the *Nine Ways of Prayer of Saint Dominic*, we have an impressive example of a man bringing his whole self—mind, heart, and spirit—into a place of reflection and prayer, a man obviously at ease with God and therefore unafraid to express whatever thoughts and feelings might happen to arise. "It was as if," we read, "he were arguing with a friend, at one moment he would appear to be feeling impatient, nodding his head energetically, then he would seem to be listening quietly, then you would see him disputing and struggling . . . then again speaking quietly and beating his breast."[14]

Though Dominic, we are told, has sat down to read a book, he is clearly not engaged in formal study. It's more like meditation or *lectio divina*. Nevertheless, the space, the reverence, that Dominic lends here to his own thoughts and feelings in the search for God should, I think, encourage those of us involved in the task of study not to dismiss as somehow distracting or unimportant the questions that likewise rise up from the weight and pressure of our own experience. It is allowing for this kind of personal engagement with the authority and genius of the great tradition that, more than anything else, helps transform the dogged task of study into an adventure.

KNOWLEDGE INTO WISDOM

Nowadays, we find ourselves surrounded by many new forms of learning and social media, all of them vying for our attention: web pages, audio files, YouTube, Twitter, Facebook, and so on. We are witnessing what has been called, and for good reason, an "information explosion." It is a virtual "tsunami" of *knowing*. And yet all the information in the world will never add up to that illumined knowledge, both simple and profound, that we call wisdom. Many years ago, the poet T.S. Eliot posed a question that remains, I believe, as sharp and relevant as ever:

14. "The Eighth Way of Prayer" of *The Nine Ways of Prayer of Saint Dominic*, in *Early Dominicans*, 101.

Where is the wisdom we have lost in knowledge?
Where is the knowledge we have lost in information?[15]

Wisdom, you could say, is knowledge that goes straight into the bloodstream and changes people's lives. It affects their whole being. And that, needless to say, is the kind of knowledge that transformed the lives and writings of the Dominican saints we most admire. If, at this moment, we were able to speak directly with Aquinas and ask him how he was able to become such a great student, such a truly profound man of wisdom, I have no doubt that he would give the same answer he gave centuries ago to his Dominican brothers—namely, that "prayer and the help of God had been of greater help to him in the search for truth than his natural intelligence and habit of study."[16]

Wisdom is the knowledge that's most critical when it comes to the apostolate of preaching and teaching. So how, then, should we prepare ourselves to receive that gift, that grace? Is there a way, a practice, that can help bring about the transformation of knowledge into wisdom? The answer is, of course, one that you know well. It is the humble day-to-day practice of private prayer and, with that, keeping faith day-to-day with the ordinary Dominican practice of communal prayer.

The preacher's task is succinctly, brilliantly summed up in the phrase *contemplata aliis tradere*—passing on to others things contemplated.[17] Part of that task, a huge part, involves the acquiring,

---

15. T.S. Eliot, "Chorus from the Rock," in *Complete Poems and Plays* (London: Harcourt, 1952), 96.

16. Bernard Gui, *The Life of St. Thomas Aquinas* 15, in *The Life of Saint Thomas Aquinas: Biographical Documents*, ed. Kenelm Foster (London: Longmans, 1959), 3.

17. *ST* 3.40.1 ad 2.

through devoted study, of knowledge about the Gospel that we are then happy and willing to communicate to others. But that does not describe the entirety of the task—far from it. For the phrase *contemplata aliis tradere*, if not understood properly, can easily give the impression, the *mistaken* impression, that preachers, as they reflect on the mysteries of faith, remain in supreme and complete control of the process, sitting at their desk, as it were, and taking down educated notes on the Gospel in order to pass the information on to others.

In the preparation for preaching, however, there comes a point when something more is demanded of us as preachers. For honest prayer sooner or later requires that, during the time of prayer, we move out of our comfort zone and are willing, after the manner of St. Dominic at prayer, to take a risk. It requires that I stand before God just as I am, naked and desiring, vulnerable and needy. This will involve, yes, a definite seeking of God on my part and a contemplation of God. But it will also involve, and far more importantly, God contemplating me, God's light and love and power impacting my heart and soul, my mind and senses. Far more important, therefore, than my seeking God is the fact that God is seeking me, God is searching my heart, God is testing my heart, God is making demands on the preacher.

Of the many challenges facing us today as preachers, perhaps the most demanding of all is the call to go into the gap of prayer and somehow to find courage to stand still in the radiance of the divine scrutiny, exposed in all our human frailty and brokenness. It is there in that place, which can seem and feel at times so completely dark and cold and empty, that the light and the fire have their source—the light of the knowledge of God and the fire of the grace of preaching.

Earlier, I made reference to the scholars at the time of Jesus who had failed to benefit from the great opportunity given to them to seize hold of "the key of knowledge." In contrast, what has impressed me over the years regarding the student friars who have come to Rome for further studies is that, almost without exception, they have been more than willing to seize with both hands the opportunity given to them by the Order. If, however, there is one criticism to be made—and it's a criticism I make of myself—it's that sometimes we focus so intensely on our academic tasks that we risk overlooking other key challenges and other needs, not least among them the need for constant, dedicated prayer. After all our years of study in Rome, it would be a real pity if we returned home to our provinces decidedly more informed than before, yes, and more knowledgeable, yes, and more manifestly clever, but not perhaps an iota more wise!

No one was more dedicated to study than Brother Thomas d'Aquino. But he remained all his life a man of profound and humble devotion. He clearly understood that a life exclusively devoted to the task of study was a life at risk. According to one of his contemporaries, Bernard Gui, "in order to offset the aridity which is so often the result of abstract and subtle speculative thinking," Brother Thomas would devote a certain amount of time to reading works that speak more to the heart than to the head, texts, for example, from the Desert Fathers.[18] This humble practice, Gui goes on to say, "did both his heart good by increasing devotion and his intellect by deepening its considerations."[19]

18. Gui, *Life of St. Thomas Aquinas* 15, p. 38.
19. Gui, 38.

When a scholar adopts an exclusively scientific or academic approach to both life and work, almost inevitably the result is an unhappy dullness and dryness of spirit, an atrophy of the faculties. This happened two centuries ago to the great English scientist Charles Darwin. In his autobiography, he makes the following startling admission: "My mind seems to have become a kind of machine for grinding general laws out of large collections of facts."[20] What a grim fate for a scholar! We can only hope and pray that no Thomist, young or old, will ever find himself adopting such a cold, machine-like approach to the adventure of study and research.

With regard to intellectual pursuits in general, it is of course required of us that we are as rigorously scientific as possible and as knowledgeable as possible also regarding the saving doctrines of the orthodox Catholic tradition. But something else is required, especially if we are called to be preachers. It is something to which St. John Paul II has drawn particular attention. In his semi-autobiographical work *Donum et Mysterium*, he writes, "The minister of the Word must possess and pass on that knowledge of God which is not a mere deposit of doctrinal truths but a personal and living experience of the mystery."[21]

All of us are aware, I think, of the gap that exists between mere academic knowledge and the knowledge that is living faith experience. What has always impressed me about the teachers and preachers in the Order of Dominic whom I most admire is that, although all of them, like ourselves, experienced in the beginning the sharp, humbling awareness of the gap "between knowing and

20. Quoted in *Charles Darwin: His Life Told in an Autobiographical Chapter and in a Selected Series of his Published Letters,* ed. Francis Darwin (New York: D. Appleton, 1893), 54.
21. John Paul II, *Gift and Mystery: On the 50th Anniversary of My Priestly Ordination* (New York: Image Books, 1996), 111.

knowing with all one's soul,"[22] they learned with God's help, over a lifetime of surrender to the demands of study, fraternal life, and the life of prayer, to abolish that distance.

WISDOM AND THE CROSS

It is prayer, as has been noted already, that more than anything else helps transform knowledge into wisdom. But there is something else as well that can achieve, I believe, that same kind of transformation. It is the reality of the cross in our lives. St. John Henry Newman says of the preacher that if he has never really suffered in his life, he will almost inevitably preach superficial sermons, using the Word of God "for his own purposes."[23] In effect, he will be talking about himself. Newman then goes on to remark, and his words are memorable, "But let his heart at length be ploughed by some keen grief or deep anxiety, and Scripture is a new book to him."[24]

The difficulties and challenges we experience as student friars here in Rome, though they may seem slight compared with the sufferings of others, are nonetheless very real. For some, the trial is the fact of living away from home in a foreign country and being bereft, therefore, of the normality of an active Dominican apostolate. For others, the trial may be the studies themselves, the challenge of coping with new and difficult subjects and also—let's admit it—with new and sometimes difficult professors! I find it encouraging to note here that Thomas Aquinas himself faced challenges of his own as a young student friar. A manuscript has survived in Thomas' hand, a

22. A phrase from the French philosopher Gustave Thibon. It occurs in his introduction to *Gravity and Grace* by Simone Weil, trans. Arthur Wills (New York: Putnam, 1952), 5.

23. John Henry Newman, *An Essay in Aid of a Grammar of Assent* (London: Burns & Oates, 1874), 62.

24. Newman, 62.

fragment of a copy by Thomas of a commentary composed by Albert the Great on Pseudo-Dionysius.[25] In thirty-eight lines of manuscript, there are a surprising number of errors made by Thomas. At one point, the young scholar even leaves out an entire line! What we are witnessing here is the great Aquinas as a fallible young student, a young man devoted to his task but, like the rest of us, not always able to get it right!

A wise Dominican remarked to me years ago that if a brother has a problem of some kind, no matter what it is, and if he comes to Rome for studies, Rome will bring that problem to the surface. Well, it's an exaggeration, of course, but there might just be something in it all the same. Finding ourselves away from the ordinary, happy pressure of the apostolate at home, it's no surprise if we begin to feel as if our lives are somehow suspended. As a result, we can be hit by a new and unexpected sense of vulnerability and, along with that, by a few piercing shocks of self-knowledge. This can be humbling, of course, but the new knowledge gained in the process can, I suggest, be as critically important as all the new academic knowledge we have been acquiring.

The struggles we face day-to-day in our lives and in our studies, and even actual failures on occasion to achieve our academic goals, might in the end be of as much value as our achievements. Why? Because they help to awaken within us a grace of attention to others. Our difficulties, Aquinas points out in the *Summa*, help us to grieve over others' misfortunes as if they were our own. Very different, he says, are those people who are always successful, "those who regard

25. Leonard Boyle discusses this particular manuscript in his essay "St. Thomas Aquinas and the Third Millennium." See *Omnia disce: Medieval Studies in Memory of Leonard Boyle, OP*, eds. Anne J. Duggan, Joan Greatrex, and Brenda Bolton (New York: Routledge, 2005), 294–295.

themselves as so fortunate and powerful as to imagine that no evil can befall them: such have no pity." And Thomas concludes, "Thus it is always some want in us that moves us to mercy [*semper defectus est ratio miserendi*]."[26]

It is natural, of course, to pray that this "defect" be removed. St. Paul, we know, suffered what he called "a thorn in his flesh." Three times he begged the Lord to be freed from it but without success (see 2 Cor. 12:7–9). God the Father, addressing Paul's dilemma directly in *The Dialogue* of St. Catherine of Siena, makes the following remarkable declaration:

> Could I and can I not make it otherwise for Paul and the others in whom I leave this or that sort of pricking? Yes. Then why does my providence do this? To give them opportunity for merit, to keep them in the self-knowledge whence they draw true humility, to make them compassionate instead of cruel toward their neighbors so that they will sympathize with them in their labors. For those who suffer themselves are far more compassionate to the suffering than are those who have not suffered.[27]

WISDOM AND JOY

If Aquinas were here with us this morning and giving the talk, what would he say to us? Well, he would, I have no doubt, encourage us to devote ourselves wholeheartedly to the task of study and to make of it as much as possible a joy and an adventure. But Thomas would also point out to us, as he does in the *Summa*, that there are times

26. *ST* 2-2.30.2.
27. Catherine of Siena, *The Dialogue* 145, trans. Suzanne Noffke (New York: Paulist, 1980), 305.

when we need to stop and "slacken the tension of mental study."[28] Otherwise, study might well become for us no more than a drudgery and an oppression. He recommends, therefore, by way of a break, whatever it is that gives us the most obvious pleasure and delight. In our case, what comes to mind immediately are things like sport, or listening to music, or going for a hike in the hills around Rome. I would add to that list finding time also to read outside of one's own limited field of academic interest, reading great literature, for example, great novels and poetry, and in that way keeping fresh the springs of the heart and the imagination.

When the Irish Dominican Leonard Boyle was a student at Oxford many years ago, he came upon a text in Hugh of St. Victor that encouraged him to keep his mind and heart open to worlds outside his own field of specialization. That text, in the original Latin, can now be seen inscribed on Boyle's tomb in the Basilica of San Clemente here in Rome. In Latin, the text begins *Omnia disce*. In English translation, it reads, "Learn everything. Afterwards you will discover that nothing is wasted. A narrow science is no fun."[29] The mention of "fun" is telling. It's perhaps an unexpected but key ingredient in Dominican spirituality from the very beginning. It's there in the *Vitae Fratrum*, and it's there in the *Summa*. So Aquinas was completely and happily in line with the Dominican spirit and tradition when, in the *Summa,* he took to task those people who are so serious about themselves that they never say anything laughable or funny (*nec ipsi dicunt aliquid ridiculum*) but instead are always

28. *ST* 2-2.168.2.
29. Hugh of St. Victor, *Didascalicon* 6.3, trans. Franklin T. Harkins, in *Interpretation of Scripture: Theory: A Selection of Works*, ed. Franklin T. Harkins and Frans van Liere (New York: New City, 2013), 166.

trying to obstruct the fun or the amusement of others.[30] Such people are not only unpleasant company, according to Thomas, but are also morally suspect. He writes, "Those who are lacking in fun, and who never say anything ridiculous or humorous, but instead give grief to those who make jokes, not accepting even the modest fun of others, are morally unsound [in Latin, *vitiosi*]."[31]

* * *

This morning, we are here together on retreat. If we were in a classroom and not on retreat, there are many things that Thomas Aquinas would no doubt want to say to us. But, for the moment, I think it's worth asking ourselves what Thomas would like to say here and now if invited to speak? As it happens, there is one particular sentence that comes to mind. It's from Thomas' commentary on St. Paul's Letter to the Philippians. Thomas chooses on occasion to paraphrase Paul, but on this occasion he goes even further and actually extends the text, betraying the strength and depth of his passion as scholar and preacher to communicate to others—to ourselves in this case—something of the tremendous grace and freedom he experiences in knowing Christ Jesus: "I long for you to be in the very heart [literally "in the entrails"] of Christ Jesus, that is, in order that you may love him intimately, and that you may be loved by him; for human life consists in this."[32]

---

30. *ST* 2-2.168.4.
31. *ST* 2-2.168.4.
32. *Compendium theologiae*, 2.2, S. Thomae Aquinatis Opera omnia, vol. 42 (Leonine edition).